Mainstreaming Language Arts and Social Studies

Mainstreaming Language Arts and Social Studies:
SPECIAL IDEAS AND ACTIVITIES FOR THE WHOLE CLASS

Anne H. Adams
Duke University

Charles R. Coble
East Carolina University

Paul B. Hounshell
University of North Carolina
at Chapel Hill

Goodyear Publishing Company, Inc.   Santa Monica, California

Library of Congress Cataloging in Publication Data

Adams, Anne H
 Mainstreaming language arts and social studies.

 Companion vol. to the authors' Mainstreaming science
and mathematics.

 1. Language arts (Elementary) 2. Social sciences—
Study and teaching (Elementary) I. Coble, Charles R.,
joint author. II. Hounshell, Paul B., joint author.
III. Title.

LB1576.A386 372.6'044 76-13164

ISBN 0-87620-598-8

Current printing (last digit):
10 9 8 7 6 5 4 3 2 1

ISBN: 0-87620-598-8 (P)
   0-87620-591-0 (C)
   Y-5988-4 (P)
   Y-5910-8 (C)

Book production by Ken Burke & Associates

Project editor: Judith Fillmore
Text and cover designer: Christy Butterfield
Illustrator: Nancy Freeman
Compositor: CBM Type

Printed in the United States of America

To Ann, Diana, Lois, and Mac

Preface

Before mainstreaming, elementary teachers had in their classes students displaying a wide range of abilities. After mainstreaming, in most classes, the range became wider. This book is written for elementary teachers who want to improve their strategies for working with a wide variety of students' abilities and interests. This variety now includes students formerly assigned all day to special-education classes.

Dedicated teachers are concerned with how best to minimize lines of division between regular classroom students and special-education students. They request ideas that help bring these students together and avoid situations that make the differences more marked than is absolutely necessary. Just as importantly, they want a curriculum that moves *all* students forward during the year—in academics, in accepting responsibility, in working with others, and in understanding their own actions and thoughts.

This book marks a new day in instruction suggestions for the following reasons:

No compartmentalization—No longer is it realistic to mark one set of ideas "Special Education" and another set "Other Fifth-Grade Students." Therefore, this book is *not* designed just for exceptional children and it is *not* designed only for other elementary students. It is intended for *all* students in any elementary class, and it is intended to be taught by the professional teacher.

No author-determined or test-determined grade level—Although many of the ideas in this book can be used with junior-high students, the thrust is elementary level. Children frequently surprise teachers. In researching activities for this book, we found students who easily completed lessons when all prior indications were that they would not be able to do them. On the other hand, some of the apparently easier activities were difficult for students who where supposed to "sail through" them with ease. *No one can accurately predict which lessons students can and cannot do well.* At the Duke University Reading Center, where many of these ideas were used with students ranging from retarded to gifted, the major conclusion reached was that one cannot teach students unless one exposes them to the content. Similar results were found in the reactions of teachers and students at the University of North Carolina at Chapel Hill and at East Carolina University. Therefore, this book has no grade limits; that determination is not nearly as important as what takes place between teacher and student.

A wide, rather than restricted, learning base—Obviously, every student will not complete every activity in this book; however, the philosophy in this book is to present numerous teaching ideas. An individual student cannot and should not be pressured to learn too much in a short period of time, but the opposite situation places the educator in a dilemma. Slow-paced, highly repetitious lessons are usually deadly. We have chosen many ideas for teachers to select from, rather than a few ideas for teachers to try to stretch. We have found that most teachers do not overload their students. Consider this book a treasure chest of teaching ideas, and pace the activities according to professional judgment.

Print and paper as major tools—It is quite popular in education today to ask teachers to use a variety of materials and teaching strategies—and most teachers do. In this book we have not emphasized the use of film, tapes, records, transparencies, etc. because we find most teachers are using these devices. We enthusiastically endorse using audiovisual materials, and there is an unwritten assumption that audiovisual materials will be used in the classroom. This book deals directly with activities for students to do using printed materials, paper, pencil, and chalkboard. We have attempted to minimize educational jargon in the book and to direct the teacher's attention to purpose, material, and possible lesson procedure.

A joy in teaching and learning—Although the book is well stocked with ideas, the real purpose is to transmit exciting learning signals to students. Only by creating situations in which different kinds of learning can take place can today's teacher hope to make great strides in instruction. Real life itself is filled with numerous series of short-term and long-term activities, with variety and with a multitude of "things." Children labeled as emotionally disturbed or perceptually handicapped should not be denied the excitement of creative and basic school-type activities; rather, all students should be given numerous content-area themes to investigate.

Specific instructional design—We find most teachers want teaching suggestions in a succinct fashion, and simply do not have time to wade through excess words. The book format is deliberately to the point, and loaded with practical ideas that apply to exceptional children working in classrooms with other children. In essence, this book is a compilation of activities emphasizing the content through which processes are oriented. Because of the variety of information, materials, individual and group techniques, etc., the threat of boredom is minimized, and the keynote is placed where it should be: transmitting knowledge, developing skills, and initiating interests. Although we realize that there are other kinds of teaching materials, we place an educational value on items that historically have served well in the classroom: paper, books, other printed materials, pencils, chalk, and chalkboard.

Time-span objectives—Individual student objectives for each theme are identified on a daily basis, rather than by week, month, or semester; the theme objectives are presented on a weekly basis. The teacher should decide how much of the week, as well as how much of the day, to devote to various aspects of the theme. Research undertaken in preparation of this book revealed that, contrary to some practices, educators do not have unlimited time to teach exceptional children. The point is not how many times an idea is repeated, or how many lessons are spent on getting ideas across to students, but rather how well a student wants to do and can do many different kinds of activities. Instead of negative planning, or not progressing until mastery is achieved, this book advocates a positive span of objectives within the realistic framework of the academic week. The theme builds during the week in an effort to accommodate the various abilities of students in the classroom. Some will zero in on the concept on Monday; others will grasp it on Friday; still others will need additional time. The decision is then left to the teacher as to whether to continue the theme for additional time or to initiate a new theme, and this can only be the teacher's decision.

We wish to thank Christy Butterfield for the book design and Nancy Freeman for the illustrations used in the book. We also wish to thank Kathleen Burroughs, Karen Collier, and Jean Taylor for typing the manuscript.

The companion volume to this book is *Mainstreaming Science and Mathematics*.

Anne H. Adams
Charles R. Coble
Paul B. Hounshell

Contents

Part Two Social Studies

Mainstreaming Language Arts and Social Studies

Language Arts

Language Arts

1 Learning Names of People in the Classroom

2 Using the Telephone for Pleasure, Safety, and Business

3 Reading Different Signs and Symbols

4 Recognizing Language Power

5 Recognizing Printed Context Clues

6 Following Printed Directions

7 Noting Prefixes and Suffixes

8 Using References

9 Beginning Sentences for Different Purposes

10 Emphasizing the Importance of Phrases

11 Improving Spelling of "Survival" Words

12 Identifying and Using Compound Words

13 Emphasizing Phonics in Classroom and Home

14 Detecting Main Ideas

15 Getting Information from Paragraphs

16 Identifying Nouns and Verbs

17 Improving Voice Communication

18 Using Sentences Effectively

1

General Overview Special-education students need to learn to associate their names in different handwritings and print forms with usage in everyday life. The self-concept factors involved with a child's name cannot be overestimated, and the teacher should encourage each student to identify his or her name in a positive manner, with the added element of identification of one's name with implications of its use.

Learning Objectives During the first week, each student will read and write his or her own name, not only in isolation but also with reference to specific instances in which a person's name is commonly used. In addition, the students will learn to read the names of classmates.

MON

Objective Recognizing one's name in different print forms.

Teacher Preparation Give each student a four-by-six-inch card with his or her name written on the card in both manuscript and cursive handwriting, paper, paste, or tape.

Activities Students tear letters from newspapers to form their names. Encourage students to locate names in all uppercase (capital) letters, first letter capitalized and other letters not capitalized. Paste letters on the card.

TUES

Objective Recognizing one's name in a telephone book and locating a friend's name in an alphabetical list, such as a telephone book.

Teacher Preparation Give each student a page torn from an outdated telephone book. The page should be stapled to a stencil of the alphabetical listing of each *last name* of students.

Activities Discuss the factors of alphabetizing and of last names placed first in the telephone book. Ask each student to complete the stencil list by writing in first names of classmates. Encourage students to refer to a posted list of first and last names of students.

WED

Objective Contrasting times for signing first names with occasions for signing full names.

Teacher Preparation Give each student a stencil containing the following: a grocery list, a formal thank-you note, a request for information from a business, a memo to a parent.

Activities Ask each student to read the items on the stencil and to write his or her first name only or first and last name, depending on the nature of the message.

THURS

FRI

Objective   Associating a person's name with a news story.

Teacher Preparation   Collect one-sentence "news" information from every student in the class. Place the information on a stencil, omitting the first name of each student. Distribute to each child.

Activities   Students read the newspaper and write in the appropriate blank the last name of each student. (*Note:* All students should be included.)

Objective   Learning to write one's name on different kinds of forms.

Teacher Preparation   Students assist the teacher in cutting forms from magazines. Give each student at least two different forms.

Activities   Each student completes at least the name item on each form given. The emphasis is on writing the name clearly—within the space allocated.

2

General Overview Although the telephone has become one of the most frequently used intermediaries in today's society, many students do not know the basic steps in using the instrument effectively. For example, in the event of a fire at home, how many would know how to locate the telephone number of the fire department? The teacher should contact the local telephone company for brochures and classroom demonstrations.

Learning Objectives Each student will learn how to use the telephone for three major purposes: (1) personal conversations, (2) emergencies, and (3) business information. All three areas are essential to effective communication via common technology.

MON

Objective Learning to dial local telephone numbers.

Teacher Preparation Provide each student with one page of numbers taken from the white pages of an outdated telepone book and a mock telephone dial made from construction paper and a brad.

Activities Students "dial" (1) the first number of the page, (2) the last number on the page, and (3) the number of the first business listed in larger print on the page. In each instance, they write the telephone number and read to a partner the name and address given.

TUES

Objective Learning to locate emergency telephone numbers.

Teacher Preparation Give each student a stencil copy of police, fire, poison control, state highway patrol, and other selected emergency numbers *as shown* on that page in the directory. Let each student see the original page during class.

Activities Students circle the appropriate number on the stencil copy as the teacher says "police," "fire," etc. Have a discussion of the meaning of illegal misuse of the telephone, such as profane language, threats, harassing calls, unnecessary calls, etc.

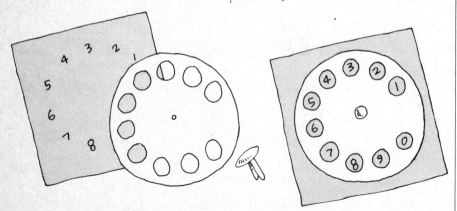

WED

Objective Learning to locate area codes for different localities.

Teacher Preparation Give each student an outline map of the United States, or point to specific states on a wall map. Provide one copy of the area-code map found in the telephone book for each small group of students.

Activities Students refer to the area-code map found in the telephone book and locate the following area codes:

1. Code(s) in the state
2. Codes in at least two adjoining states
3. Codes in other states in which relatives live
4. Codes in other states in which members of the group have lived

Discuss how to use area code in dialing long distance, and if it is required for in-state dialing.

THURS

Objective Learning to use alphabetical listing in the yellow pages.

Teacher Preparation Provide each small group of students with at least four yellow pages from the telephone book. The pages should not be in alphabetical order.

Activities Students (1) put the pages in alphabetical order; (2) circle key words in advertisements; (3) discuss services provided by different businesses as advertised in the yellow pages. (*Note:* A variation is to instruct students to cut yellow-page advertisements in blocks and paste the ads in alphabetical order according to business heading.)

FRI

Objective Learning to locate selected kinds of business telephone numbers in the yellow pages.

Teacher Preparation Cut the advertisement displays for businesses from the yellow pages. Place the line item for each business on paper.

Activities Students match the business line item with the corresponding advertisement. They then circle the telephone number appearing in both the line item and in the advertisement. A group project is to make a booklet of businesses students have visited.

Notes

3

General Overview Symbols are found in numerous forms and meanings in society. Students should learn to read these symbols readily. Sign-reading lessons initiated during the third week should be expanded throughout the year to include other symbols. When students bring a copy of a symbol or sign to class, it should be placed on the chalkboard and a discussion of its meaning(s) should be held.

Learning Objectives Each student will learn to read a variety of signs and symbols, with emphasis on those commonly found in stores, on labels, on streets and highways, and denoting different occupations.

MON

Objective Learning to read common signs in stores.

Teacher Preparation When in different stores, note various signs. Place these on the chalkboard.

Activities Students learn to read the signs and discuss their meaning. For today's lesson, the following are recommended: SALE, ESCALATOR, ELEVATOR, PERSONNEL ONLY, WOMEN, MEN, EXIT, TELEPHONE, MANAGER.

TUES

Objective Learning to read symbols on food labels.

Teacher Preparation Give each group of students at least four labels or packages removed from canned, frozen, or dried foods.

Activities Students circle *on the labels* the answers—including signs, symbols, and abbreviations—for the following questions:

1. How much does the food weigh?
2. What is the name of the state in which the product was made?
3. Do other signs, symbols, or abbreviations appear on the label?

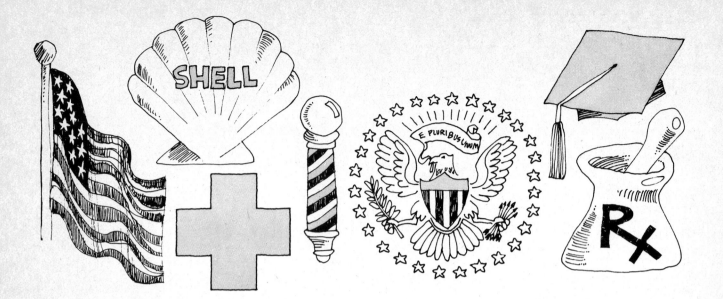

WED

Objective Learning to read signs on streets.

Teacher Preparation Provide each student with a copy of common street signs.

Activities Students discuss the meanings of the signs, such as MAIN STREET, PEDESTRIAN CROSSING, and ONE-WAY TRAFFIC.

THURS

Objective Learning to read highway markers.

Teacher Preparation Provide each group of students with the illustrated pages of signs in the state highway-safety department's driver-education book.

Activities Students discuss the meaning of the signs, such as STOP, RAILROAD CROSSING, YIELD, NO U-TURN, etc.

FRI

Objective Learning to associate symbols with the appropriate occupation.

Teacher Preparation Provide students with a copy of the symbols above. Give each group of students copies of the yellow pages from the telephone book.

Activities Students associate the symbol and occupation, and discuss related services. Each group of students makes a booklet of local business symbols (motel, appliance, restaurant, etc.), using advertisements from the yellow pages of the telephone book. Students circle the symbols.

Notes

Recognizing Language Power

4

General Overview Various devices are used in printed and oral language to emphasize ideas. Whether for purposes of emphasis, promotion, or general information, students should be aware of different power devices used in language. Although useful in all situations, these lessons are particularly valuable in consumer education.

Learning Objectives Each student will learn to recognize various shades of emphasis employed in both spoken and printed language. Particular emphasis is on influences in language used in magazines, newspapers, informal conversation, fiction and nonfiction books, and radio and television.

MON

Objective Recognizing influential words in magazines.

Teacher Preparation Provide each group of three students with a magazine.

Activities Students circle words for each of the following: (1) the largest, most colorful words in advertisements; (2) the titles of articles as contrasted with the first sentence; and (3) boldface words in articles. For each, the students discuss reasons for the words circled.

TUES

Objective Noting major words in newspapers.

Teacher Preparation Provide each group of three students with the first page of a newspaper.

Activities Students circle responses to each of the following: (1) the largest group of words on the page (lead headline); (2) names of persons in photograph captions; (3) second largest group of words on the page (secondary headlines). Students discuss reasons these groups of words received emphasis.

WED

Objective Detecting emphasis words in conversations.

Teacher Preparation Provide each group of three students with a topic that can be debated from opposing points of view.

Activities One student expresses opinions of the advantages of the topic. The second student in the group takes the opposite viewpoint. The third student takes notes of words that receive emphasis. For the next two topics, a different student takes notes. Topics recommended for this lesson are:

1. Children should/should not do chores at home.
2. Children should/should not have a set time to go to bed.
3. Children should/should not have homework each night.

THURS

Objective Locating strategic words in stories and nonfiction.

Teacher Preparation Ask each student to select a library book.

Activities Students locate one sentence in the book and note the most important two words in that sentence. Each student should have a reason for the words selected. As an extension, ask students to find quotations or explanations of an item or idea.

FRI

Objective Recognizing power words on radio and television.

Teacher Preparation Provide a transistor radio and/or television set in the classroom. Each student should have paper and pencil. If a television set is used, the screen should be darkened or covered so only the sound is transmitted.

Activities Students listen to commercials and indicate words that receive vocal emphasis. Either the teacher or students record these words. Later, discuss why these words received emphasis.

Notes

Recognizing Printed Context Clues

General Overview The context clue is the most frequently available indicator of the meaning given to a specific word. Such clues are usually found in the same sentence when the word is introduced; however, the clue may be given later. Since people do not always use a dictionary, lessons in detecting context clues should be held frequently during the year. An introductory emphasis on context clues is suggested for the fifth week. It is important that lessons on locating context clues be held in *each* of the content areas studied.

Learning Objectives Each student will recognize printed context clues in a variety of situations, including textbooks, advertisements, and newspapers.

MON

Objective Locating context clues in mathematics textbooks.

Teacher Preparation Locate the sentence(s) in the mathematics textbook where two specialized mathematics words in today's lesson are explained in the context of the sentences.

Activities Students write the context clues for the two specialized words as found in the sentences. Students then circle the most important words in the context clues.

Notes

TUES

Objective Spotting context clues in advertisements.

Teacher Preparation Provide each pair of students with two advertisements taken from either magazines or newspapers.

Activities Students circle the context clue words that pertain *only* to the product being advertised. Students then exchange advertisements with other students. Each checks to make sure the words circled are clues to the product rather than items not specifically describing the meaning or uses of the product.

WED

Objective Locating context clues in social-studies textbooks.

Teacher Preparation Locate the sentence(s) in the social-studies textbook where two vocabulary words in today's lesson are explained in context within the sentence.

Activities Students write the context clues for the two specialized words as found in the sentences. Students then circle the most important words in the context clues.

THURS

Objective Underlining context clues in newspaper articles.

Teacher Preparation Provide each student with a newspaper article wherein at least one context clue is included to define a technical word used or the name of an organization.

Activities Students locate and underline the context clue. They then circle the word(s) or name of organization being defined and draw an arrow from the context clue to the word(s).

FRI

Objective Locating context clues in science textbooks.

Teacher Preparation Locate the sentence(s) in the science textbook where two specialized science words in today's lesson are explained in context.

Activities Students write the context clues for the two specialized words as found in the sentences. Students then circle the most important words in the context clues.

6

General Overview The importance of correctly following printed directions cannot be overstated, and at least one week of lessons emphasizing this language-arts area should be included in the year. During the sessions, a variety of different kinds of printed directions should be available to the students.

Learning Objectives Each student will read and respond to directions pertaining to map reading, cooking, constructing at least one item, playing games, and reading directions for science experiences.

MON

Objective Following instructions pertaining to travel directions.

Teacher Preparation Provide each student with a three-inch-square segment of a local or state road map, and a list of directions to follow.

Activities Students read the map and write responses to the directions. Directions recommended for today's lesson, if road map segments are used, are:

1. Pretend you are driving from the largest town on your map
2. Write the names of the towns you will travel through if you go fifty miles north.
3. Write the name of the nearest lake or river where you will spend a weekend fishing. Write the name of a town on that river or lake.
4. How many miles would you drive to a city that would have more than 100,000 people living in it?

TUES

Objective Constructing an item by following printed directions.

Teacher Preparation Explain to the students that each is to write the directions for another student to make an item from paper and paste.

Activities Each student writes the directions for making a paper-paste object and exchanges directions with another student. If directions are incomplete, the student is to ask the writer of the directions to clarify information.

WED

Objective Noting steps in recipes.

Teacher Preparation Provide each student with a copy of a recipe. The ingredients should be listed above the cooking steps.

Activities If not numbered, the student first numbers the steps in the recipe. The student then writes the step number beside each item in the list of ingredients. In small groups, discuss what might happen if the ingredients were combined out of order.

11

THURS | FRI

Objective Playing a game by following written directions.

Teacher Preparation Provide each group of students with directions for playing a game. The games might be commercial or invented by the teacher or students.

Activities Each group of students follows the written directions to play the game.

Objective Initiating a science experiment by following written directions.

Teacher Preparation Locate in the science textbook one experiment for each group of students to read the directions and complete the experiment.

Activities Students read instructions in the textbook and complete the science experiment.

Noting Prefixes and Suffixes

General Overview Prefixes and suffixes either change the meaning of base words or enhance the definitions. Studying isolated lists of prefixes and suffixes may not be as meaningful as learning about them with reference to academic and recreational information. The seventh week is an introductory emphasis on both prefixes and suffixes. Include supplementary lessons during the remainder of the year, emphasizing other prefixes and suffixes, with prefixes emphasized in separate sessions from suffixes.

Learning Objectives Each student will identify selected printed prefixes and suffixes as found in magazines, dictionaries, textbooks, and newspapers. In addition, the students will write prefixes depicting certain physical actions.

MON

Objective Locating prefixes in magazines.

Teacher Preparation Provide each pair of students with a magazine. Write prefixes such as *de, mis, un, pre, in,* and *im* on the chalkboard and briefly discuss the meaning of each.

Activities Each pair of students circles in the magazine as many words as can be found containing the selected prefixes. Consider placing a time limit on this activity.

Notes

TUES

Objective Writing prefixes for physical actions.

Teacher Preparation Place the following pairs of words on the chalkboard and discuss the effect of the prefixes: *glue, unglue; lock, unlock.*

Activities Each group of three students makes lists of words that (1) can have a prefix and (2) require some action. Students then read the base word; other students add an appropriate prefix. If time permits, students illustrate the action.

WED

Objective Locating prefixes and suffixes in a dictionary.

Teacher Preparation Provide each student or pair of students with a dictionary and a list of prefixes and suffixes, such as *re, con, sub, bi* (prefixes), and *less, ful, ing, ed* (suffixes).

Activities Students locate the dictionary definition of each prefix and suffix, and write the two words in each definition that seem the most important to the student.

FRI

Objective Locating suffixes in textbooks.

Teacher Preparation Provide each student with a copy of a content-area textbook.

Activities Students read sentences containing words that have suffixes. One student reads the sentence to another student, omitting the suffix. The partner tells which word should have a suffix. They both then note the difference in meaning when the base word containing its suffix is read in the sentence.

THURS

Objective Locating prefixes and suffixes in newspapers.

Teacher Preparation Provide each student with one newspaper page (primarily of news articles).

Activities Students, working in pairs, place a circle around each prefix and a square around each suffix. They then list the prefixes and suffixes found for later use in other language-arts lessons.

8

General Overview   There are numerous references people consult in business or recreational pursuits. For example, when moving to a new city, people may refer to classified newspaper advertisements for housing possibilities; studying the guide for nightly television programs has become almost habitual for many people. Still, there are students who are not aware of these resources or how to use them. The eighth week provides an emphasis on such references.

Learning Objectives   Each student will learn to use selected, easily found references, with emphasis on newspaper classified advertisements, catalogs, television programs, transportation schedules, and warranties.

MON

Objective   Referring to newspaper classified advertisements for information.

Teacher Preparation   Provide each small group of students with a section from the newspaper classified advertisements. (For this lesson, segments from the section on pets, housing for sale and for rent, and automobiles for sale are recommended.)

Activities   Students underline answers to questions concerning the advertisements. Questions suggested for today's lesson are:

1. What is the topic of this section?
2. What is the most expensive item in the section?
3. What is the oldest item in the section?
4. Which item would you like to have?

TUES

Objective   Using catalogs for item information.

Teacher Preparation   Provide each student with at least four pages from different sections of a catalog. (Examples: tape recorders, guitars, boats, models.)

Activities:

1. The student underlines adjectives describing the most expensive and least expensive items on one page.
2. The student circles the heaviest item on one page.
3. The student underlines the color choices for three items on one page.
4. The student compares prices of items that are pictured with descriptions and prices of items not illustrated.

WED

Objective   Reading television-program schedules.

Teacher Preparation   Provide each student with a copy of *TV Guide* or the newspaper page pertaining to television programs.

Activities   Each pair of students uses the program list and any accompanying information to complete the following:

1. Categorize one night's television programs offered on one channel under the appropriate heading of: *news, sports, comedy, mystery, history.*
2. Contrast programs listed at 8 P.M. and 9 P.M. on at least three different channels. For example, note if comedies are opposite comedies.
3. Circle the adjectives used in program descriptions of three different programs. Compare the programs.

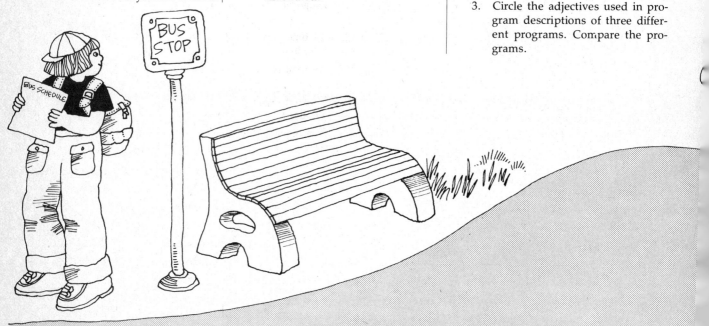

THURS

FRI

Objective Reading different kinds of transportation references, such as airline, bus, and train schedules.

Teacher Preparation Provide each student with a copy of at least a section from an airline, train, or bus schedule. Maps, globes, and, if possible, atlases should be available.

Activities Students in small groups first discuss what information is needed by people about to take a trip by commercial transportation. Then, using hypothetical destinations as printed on the group's schedule, the students note travel arrival and departure times and intermediate stops. The third activity is to pretend there was no space on the shortest route, and the group plans the next best route.

Objective Referring to warranties and warranty information for specific information.

Teacher Preparation This lesson is more effective if actual copies of warranties are used than if information is placed on stencil. The teacher may need to bring warranties of items, such as toaster, lawnmower, radio, etc., from home. Divide the class into groups of four students per group. Each group should have time to compare at least three different warranties. Mock stencil warranty cards might be used for students to complete information such as name, address, etc.

Activities The students read the warranties to locate answers to the following questions:

1. What is the time span of the warranty?
2. Are there different time limits for different parts of the item?
3. Where should one mail the warranty card?
4. What can a person do if the store does not repair the item?
5. What information is requested on the warranty card?

General Overview   The study of writing and reading sentences receives considerable attention in school; however, many students continue to write the same basic sentence structure. There is a need for emphasis on how to write different kinds of sentences and to recognize that the way a sentence is written can weaken or strengthen the writer's dissemination of information. During the ninth week, daily lessons are held concerning various ways to initiate sentences. Although students should be encouraged to complete the sentences, the emphasis is on developing an awareness of the influence of initial aspects in sentence writing and reading. These lessons should be correlated with creative writing and art.

Learning Objectives   Each student will write and respond to sentences with different types of beginnings. Students will learn to write sentences to request and to impart information; sentences beginning with prepositional phrases, descriptions, and clauses.

MON

Objective   Detecting and writing sentences requesting information.

Teacher Preparation   Provide each student with one page from a popular magazine where classified advertisements are listed.

Activities   Each student writes one sentence requesting information concerning at least four advertisements. Students use each of the following sentence beginnings, and complete the sentence with items appropriate to the product selected. When finished, the students discuss how the sentence beginnings influenced which information was requested. Suggested sentence beginnings for use in this lesson are:

1. If the product does not do what you claim it will do, what _____?

2. Why does the product _____?

3. How does the product _____?

4. When should the product ____?

TUES

Objective   Detecting and writing sentences containing information.

Teacher Preparation   Provide each student with at least one of the following from the newspaper: a front-page article about the actions of an individual, an article from the sports page, and an article from the society page.

Activities   The student locates and underlines in the article the first four words in each sentence containing answers to the following:

1. *Whom* is the article about?

2. *Where* did the first event in the article take place?

3. *When* did the event occur?

4. *What* is the main topic of the article?

Students then discuss the effects that the beginning words have on the remainder of the sentence.

WED

Objective   Writing sentences beginning with prepositional phrases.

Teacher Preparation   Give each student a stencil copy of five prepositional phrases or write the prepositional phrases on the chalkboard. Suggested for today's lesson are:

1. In the house,

2. Before the raging storm,

3. Under the kitchen table,

4. After eating twelve ice cream cones,

5. Beside the bicycle,

Activities   Students complete each sentence in writing. They then substitute prepositions and discuss different endings for the sentences. For example:

1. Before eating twelve ice cream cones,

2. Beside the house,

3. After the bicycle,

Notes

THURS

10

Objective Writing sentences with descriptive beginnings.

Teacher Preparation Place groups of two to four adjectives on the chalkboard. Place the word *and* before the last adjective in each group. Examples of adjectives are: young *and* playful; a gray, tired, wrinkled, *and* furry; the blue, wet, *and* cold . . . .

Activities Students discuss various ways to complete sentences beginning with each of the phrases. Each student then writes sentences containing each of the phrases.

General Overview As an extension to lessons held the preceding week, topics during the tenth week concentrate on the importance of phrases in communication. Students need to be aware of the influence descriptive words have in their reading, and they need to be able to select appropriate words that enhance their own writings.

Learning Objectives Each student will learn to develop phrases describing people, places, actions, intangibles, and emotions.

FRI

Objective Writing sentences beginning with clauses.

Teacher Preparation Place clauses on the chalkboard. Suggested clauses are: walking very tall; instead of thinking; pretending to be happy at the thought of going outside, ...

Activities Students discuss possible sentence endings for different specific categories. Suggested for the above topics are: a sports figure, a puppy, and a monster. Students discuss influences different categories have on sentences.

MON

Objective Selecting various words to describe people.

Teacher Preparation Provide each pair of students with a comic book or three comic strips from a newspaper.

Activities Above each character depicted in the comic, students write one word that describes one facial expression indicated in the illustration. The students then select three words and write three phrases, incorporating the word in the phrase. Examples: in an *angry* way, . . . ; . . . on the *happy* side.

TUES

Objective Selecting different phrases to describe various places.

Teacher Preparation Provide each student with a magazine.

Activities Each pair of students writes descriptive phrases on magazine illustrations of various places. Use phrases such as: *the large, old castle; six miles high in the sky; a lonely stretch of beach;* and *beside the oak tree.*

WED

Objective Describing a variety of motions and actions.

Teacher Preparation The teacher should demonstrate at least three different motions, such as clapping hands slowly, "walking" fingers across a desk, and rushing to the door.

Activities Students write one phrase describing each of the teacher's motions. Each phrase should contain at least four words. Students take turns enacting an action and taking notes.

THURS

Objective Selecting words to describe intangibles with tangibles.

Teacher Preparation Provide each student with a copy of a magazine.

Activities Students search for advertisements that contain a reference to an intangible associated with the product. They circle the words for both and draw a line connecting each. An example is: *as free as a wild stallion* in an automobile advertisement.

Notes

FRI

Objective Describing emotional responses.

Teacher Preparation Provide each student with a copy of the social-studies textbook.

Activities Students select at least five illustrations in the textbook and:

1. Write the page number of the illustration.
2. Write phrases describing the emotions that might be experienced by: (1) a person revisiting the scene after being away forty years; (2) a person working at the scene; and (3) a person on vacation at the scene.

11

General Overview   Handwritten notations involving matters such as food, clothing, shelter, and health are written each year with increasing frequency. Upper-elementary students need to know how to spell such high-frequency words so they—as well as others who may be expected to read the notes—can decipher the words. During the eleventh week, the lessons emphasizing such words should serve as springboards for other survival-type spelling words to be studied during the year.

Learning Objectives   Each student will learn to spell words that are basic to his or her survival. This week's lessons emphasize learning to spell individually selected words for food, medicine, clothing, and appliances. In addition, words often associated with telephone messages will be included.

MON

Objective   Spelling words for basic grocery items.

Teacher Preparation   Provide each student with a copy of a half- or full-page grocery advertisement from a newspaper.

Activities   Each student selects the words for five to ten different food items that he/she would like to place on a grocery shopping list. The words become that student's individual spelling words. A partner calls out the words and the student writes them. The two students check the spelling, and the student being tested studies the spelling of any words that were missed.

TUES

Objective   Spelling words denoting nonprescription medicines or supplies.

Teacher Preparation   Write on the chalkboard nonprescription medicines or supplies that students in class remember using in the past. Examples: aspirin, cough syrup, vitamins, ointments, bandages.

Activities   Each student selects the words on the chalkboard that he or she has used. Those become the individual spelling words. Students follow the study-check-study procedure described for Monday.

WED

Objective   Taking telephone messages.

Teacher Preparation   Place on the chalkboard examples of different kinds of telephone messages taken by adults. Include notes taken by the teacher at home. Suggested examples for today's lesson are:

1. *Dentist appointment—March* 3, 11 A.M.
2. Pick up *television* next *Wednesday*.
3. Sandy, *call* Joyce *before* 5 today.

Activities   Each pair of students role-plays the following: one student pretends to be four different people calling at different times of the day and leaving a message. The second student takes notes for each conversation. Major words such as those *italicized* above in each message become individual spelling words for that student. They use the study-check-study procedure described in Monday's lesson.

THURS

Objective   Associating words and numerals with different kinds of clothing.

Teacher Preparation   Provide each group of four students with a general catalog containing clothing for sale.

Activities   Each group locates the page numbers and catalog descriptions of different kinds of clothing. Each student, working alone, selects one of each item, records its price, and the appropriate size.

FRI

Objective   Spelling words that refer to appliances in the home.

Teacher Preparation   Discuss different types of large and small appliances and other electrical items used in homes—stoves, refrigerators, toasters, clocks, lamps, televisions—and how to divide these words into syllables.

Activities   Students, working in small groups, make a list of home-based electrical items, categorizing the objects according to the number of syllables. These words become spelling words for members of the group. Categorize the words according to number of syllables—one, two, or more than two syllables.

___

Notes

Identifying and Using Compound Words

12

General Overview The compound word is the technique most frequently used to combine more than one idea into a single unit. Selection of appropriate compound words stems from the categorical ideas to be disseminated. During the twelfth week, the lesson emphasizes different categories and students learn to select compound words with reference to specific idea guidelines. Students should refer to a dictionary when questions are raised whether the words selected can be in compound form.

Learning Objectives Each student will learn to select and combine words into compound words, within the framework of words associated with classroom items, conversations, living and nonliving matter, and foods.

MON

Objective Learning compound words for items in the classroom.

Teacher Preparation Briefly explain to the students the basic principle of the compound word.

Activities Students in small groups make a list of compound words by combining the names of two or more items in the classroom. Each group lists as many such compound words as possible during a timed period not to exceed five minutes. Examples are: windowpane, shoelace, bookshelf, classroom, chalkboard.

WED

Objective Recognizing compound words for living matter.

Teacher Preparation Place column headings such as *people*, *animals*, and *plants* on the chalkboard.

Activities Students in small groups select and write compound words appropriate to each of the column headings.

THURS

Objective Recognizing compound words for nonliving matter.

Teacher Preparation Place categories such as *housing*, *transportation*, and *occupations* on the chalkboard.

Activities Students in small groups select and write compound words appropriate to each of the column headings.

TUES

Objective Inserting compound words in conversations.

Teacher Preparation Ask each group of students to write five words associated with favorite hobbies or pets.

Activities Students write compound words associated with each of the five topics selected by group members. These compound words might be used in a creative writing lesson.

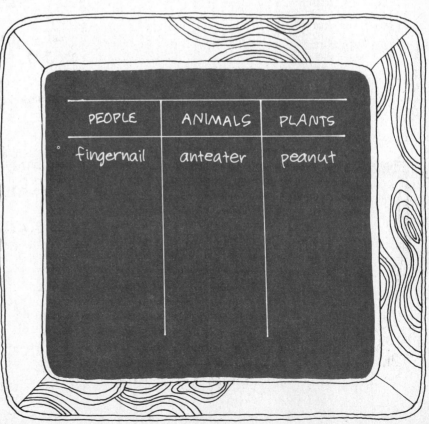

PEOPLE	ANIMALS	PLANTS
fingernail	anteater	peanut

FRI

Objective Noting compound words related to foods.

Teacher Preparation Provide each pair of students with three recipes taken from magazines, newspapers, or cookbooks.

Activities Students circle the compound words in the recipes. (Variations include circling compound words related to foods in newspaper grocery advertisements, seed catalogs, and labels from cans or jars.)

Notes

13

General Overview Although there are numerous exceptions to phonic generalizations, phonics can be useful in improving reading and spelling abilities. During this week, all phonics lessons will be associated directly with common words used in the classroom and home. No word should be studied if the students do not readily know its meaning. In the phonics lessons, the sounds should be voiced and emphasized within the word, and the letter(s) representing sounds being studied should be written by the student.

Learning Objectives Each student will associate sounds and regularly spelled letter symbols for selected words frequently used in school and home.

MON

Objective Using the sounds and letter symbols of single consonants *b* through *l*.

Teacher Preparation Place each consonant *b* through *l* on the chalkboard. For the homework part of this lesson, ask each student to locate words for items found in the kitchen and bedroom that have the sound of selected consonants.

Activities Students identify words of items in the classroom that have the sound of each of the consonants listed on the chalkboard. Students write each word on paper at their desk.

TUES

Objective Using the sounds and symbols of single consonants *m* through *z*.

Teacher Preparation Same as on Monday, except use consonants *m* through *z*.

Activities Students perform the same activities as on Monday, except one consonant can be "wild" and no word need be written beside that consonant. This will probably be the consonant *x*.

WED

Objective Using short vowel sounds and letter symbols.

Teacher Preparation Write the following on the chalkboard:

a—h*a*nd
e—b*e*ll
i—s*i*x
o—cl*o*ck
u—j*u*mp

Pronounce the short vowel sounds both in isolation and in the words.

Activities For each key word, students write other words containing the same short vowel sound.

21

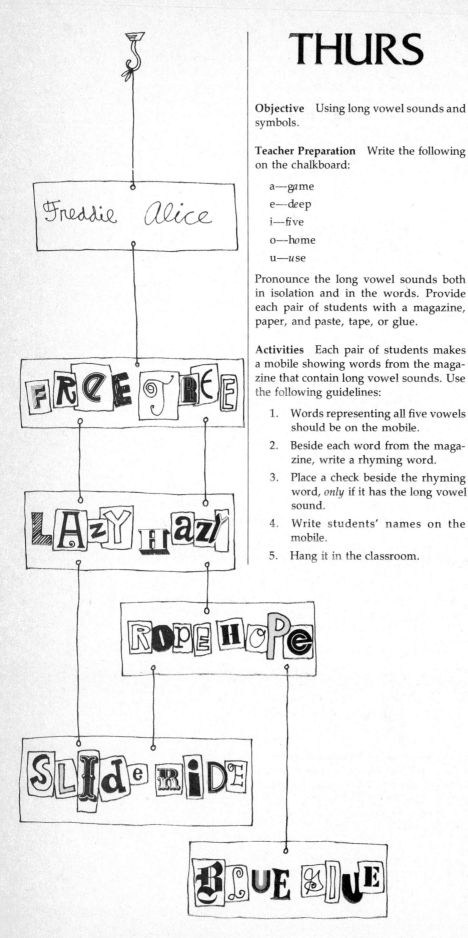

THURS

Objective   Using long vowel sounds and symbols.

Teacher Preparation   Write the following on the chalkboard:

a—g*a*me
e—d*ee*p
i—f*i*ve
o—h*o*me
u—*u*se

Pronounce the long vowel sounds both in isolation and in the words. Provide each pair of students with a magazine, paper, and paste, tape, or glue.

Activities   Each pair of students makes a mobile showing words from the magazine that contain long vowel sounds. Use the following guidelines:

1. Words representing all five vowels should be on the mobile.
2. Beside each word from the magazine, write a rhyming word.
3. Place a check beside the rhyming word, *only* if it has the long vowel sound.
4. Write students' names on the mobile.
5. Hang it in the classroom.

FRI

Objective   Using various groups of consonant clusters.

Teacher Preparation   Provide each student with a newspaper page.

Activities   Two students working together circle any consecutive group of consonants, strike through vowels in each word, and then pronounce the consonant sounds. Discuss which consonants are voiced and which are not.

Notes

General Overview Identifying main ideas communicated both in print and vocally should be encouraged, rather than asking students to detect one main idea. This week's lessons focus on the main ideas in a variety of communication devices, and for different purposes. Students need to be aware of techniques to use in locating main ideas, and discussions should be held concerning the effects of main ideas on (1) what is remembered after reading, and (2) how main ideas from one topic can relate to global themes from other topics.

Learning Objectives Each student will identify at least two main ideas gained from pictures and their captions, chapter and story titles, and phrases within sentences as well as sentences and paragraphs.

MON

Objective Locating main ideas in photographs and associating those ideas with caption information.

Teacher Preparation Provide each student with a newspaper, and ask students to locate photographs with captions. Once students complete the activity suggested below, repeat the procedure asking students to use science and social-studies textbooks.

Activities Students first study the photograph and note at least three words that indicate key ideas in the picture. They then read the picture caption to (1) detect if these words are in the caption, and (2) note which words might be considered key words in the caption.

TUES

Objective Detecting key words in chapter and story titles.

Teacher Preparation Provide each student with the table of contents from (1) a magazine, (2) a social-studies textbook, and (3) a library book.

Activities Students detect main ideas in chapter or story titles according to the contents headings, such as action stories, advice stories, chapters about places, and chapters about events, using only entries in table of contents as guides.

WED

Objective Locating main themes in phrases isolated from sentences.

Teacher Preparation Provide each student with a magazine and/or yellow pages from a telephone book.

Activities Students select phrases from advertisements. Beside each, they write at least two main ideas suggested by the phrase. One example is: "Serving this area for over fifty years" (advertisement), which students might interpret as "a good business" or "been there a long time."

THURS

Objective Identifying main ideas of sentences.

Teacher Preparation Ask students to locate only first sentences in chapters in a textbook. Refer students to the use of the table of contents to speed location of chapters.

Activities After the student reads the first sentence, he/she completes at least two blanks by writing in main ideas at this point. Then students should look at the remainder of the chapter to check their first impressions.

FRI

Objective Locating main ideas of paragraphs.

Teacher Preparation Make sure each student has access to at least ten different library books. Provide each student with ten blank cards or three-by-five-inch paper rectangles.

Activities On one side of the card, the student writes the name of the author and title of the book. On the other side of the card, the student writes the page number from which a paragraph is selected, reads the paragraph, and writes words indicating three different main ideas in that paragraph. The student exchanges cards with another student, reads the paragraphs on the page indicated, and records on the card the paragraph number in which the main ideas are presented. Students compare their ideas.

Notes

15

General Overview A part of education is becoming aware of different kinds, purposes, and styles of paragraphs. For example, a paragraph in a sports magazine usually would not be written in the same manner as in a newspaper, although both carry the same general message. Letters to friends are written in a different paragraph style than letters to businesses. During the fifteenth week, students read and write different kinds of paragraphs.

Learning Objectives Learning to read and write different styles of paragraphs, with emphasis on news reporting; direct quotes; descriptive accounts; information to friends, businesses, and agencies; and paragraphs containing conclusions.

MON

Objective Studying paragraphs containing current events.

Teacher Preparation Provide each student with a copy of a newspaper. Write headings—such as *action news, sports news, recommendation news* (boards, politicians, etc.), and *society news*—on the chalkboard.

Activities Students analyze the *third* paragraph in articles appropriate to each of the categories. They compare internal components between the different types of paragraphs, and contrast information with the first paragraphs in each story.

TUES

Objective Analyzing paragraphs containing reported conversations.

Teacher Preparation Provide each student with short stories or novels and newspaper articles containing direct quotes.

Activities Each student analyzes lead-in information as it relates to conversational information in three different paragraphs.

WED

Objective Reacting to descriptive paragraphs.

Teacher Preparation Provide each student with descriptive paragraphs in (1) a novel, (2) a social-studies textbook, and (3) a science textbook. Write the headings *who, what, when,* and *where* on the chalkboard.

Activities Students write the columns on a sheet of paper, and note descriptions in the paragraph when appropriate to the columns. For example: *who*—a young boy; *what*—a bat, banner; *when*—a sunny Friday morning; *where*—baseball park.

THURS

Objective Noting differences between paragraphs to friends and to businesses.

Teacher Preparation (1) Place the headings *friendly letter* and *business letter* on the chalkboard; (2) provide each student with a magazine.

Activities Students select one magazine advertisement and write two one-paragraph letters about the topic. In the friendly letter, they describe informally how they have used or would like to use the product. In the business letter, they formally request specific information about the product. In small groups, they compare the wordings of the two paragraphs.

FRI

Objective Observing key elements in summary paragraphs.

Teacher Preparation Provide each student with summary sections from at least three textbook chapters. Place headings on the chalkboard for: *most important ideas, next most important ideas,* and *not important ideas.*

Activities Students note at least one item for each column for each of the summary sections.

Notes

16

General Overview Selecting appropriate nouns and verbs is a key part of communication. One goal of the language-arts program is to expand the noun-verb vocabulary of students. The topics emphasized during the sixteenth week should serve as prototypes for noun-verb associations with other topics during the remainder of the academic year.

Learning Objectives Each student will use references to locate additional nouns and/or verbs for topics studied during the week.

MON

Objective Associating appropriate nouns and verbs with a hobby.

Teacher Preparation Group students according to those who share the same hobby. Provide each group with a thesaurus. Place columns on the chalkboard headed with *noun, noun, verb, verb*. In the first column, each group makes a list of nouns related to the hobby. In the third column, they list verbs related to the noun. See example below.

Activities Students then consult the thesaurus to note if a synonym for the noun and verb is included. They write the noun and verb selected in the second and fourth columns.

TUES

Objective Noting different types of nouns and verbs in current-events reporting.

Teacher Preparation Provide each student with the front page of a newspaper.

Activities Students locate at least three categories of nouns—persons, places, objects. For each, from a different section of the newspaper, they locate appropriate verbs.

WED

Objective Identifying nouns and verbs associated with television programming.

Teacher Preparation Provide each student with a copy of a television schedule.

Activities Each student selects the title of a favorite television program and writes beside the name of the program a noun describing the main character or type of program. Beside the noun, the student writes a verb describing a predominant action of the character. See example below.

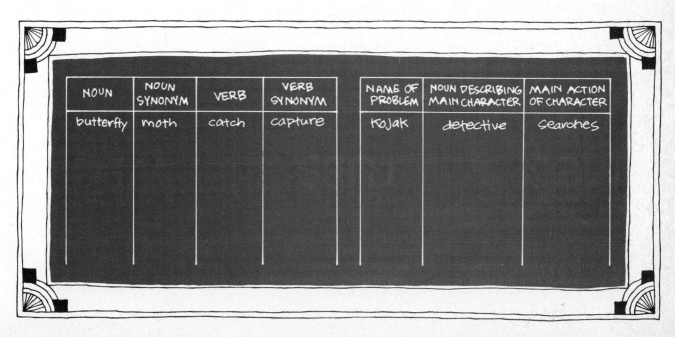

NOUN	NOUN SYNONYM	VERB	VERB SYNONYM		NAME OF PROBLEM	NOUN DESCRIBING MAIN CHARACTER	MAIN ACTION OF CHARACTER
butterfly	moth	catch	capture		Kojak	detective	searches

THURS | # FRI

Notes

Objective Associating nouns and verbs with personal health.

Teacher Preparation Each student is provided with a copy of a chart containing spaces for students to write nouns and verbs associated with food, clothing, shelter, and exercise.

Activities Beneath each column heading, the student writes one noun and verb associated with his/her experiences. See example below.

Objective Selecting appropriate nouns and verbs for finance topics.

Teacher Preparation Provide each student with a budget list that includes items such as cost of food, cost of clothing, cost of utilities, and cost of recreation.

Activities Each student estimates a one-week cost for each item. (Parents are asked to help compute this activity.)

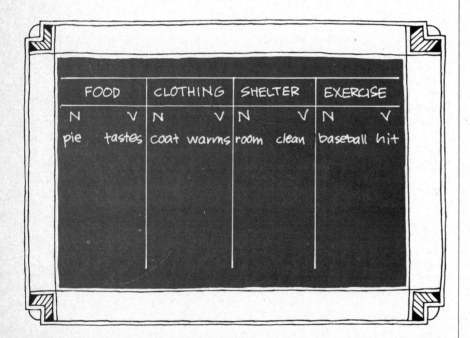

26

17

General Overview The improvement of speech in both enunciation and pronunciation obviously encompasses more than a one-week set of lessons. During the seventeenth week, however, the emphasis is on the importance of different devices for vocal communication, and how to be more effective in oral language.

Learning Objectives Each student will learn ways to improve his or her speech, particularly with response to punctuation marks, printed conversation, drama, role-playing, and vocal emphasis of key points.

MON

Objective Interpreting effects of punctuation marks.

Teacher Preparation Provide each student with an 8½-by-11-inch sheet of paper containing selected punctuation marks. Provide also a newspaper, a magazine, and paste, glue, or tape.

Activities Students cut newspaper or magazine phrases or sentences containing each of the punctuation marks, and tape the printed information in the appropriate block on the form. One student then reads the information to another student, vocally recognizing each punctuation clue.

TUES

Objective Carrying out effective conversations.

Teacher Preparation Provide each group of three students with a comic book.

Activities Each student selects a comic character, and reads the printed remarks of that character as found in quotation balloons. The students do not read aloud other information. Prior to reading, the student notes conversational words in boldface type or italics and underlines at least one additional word to emphasize in the oral reading.

WED

Objective Presenting dramatic plays.

Teacher Preparation Group students according to those who have read the same story.

Activities Each group prepares a spontaneous five- to ten-minute dramatic interpretation of the story. Use chairs, books, and tables in the classroom as props. Guidelines include: (1) each student in the group must have a speaking part; (2) a segment of the story must be given rather than the entire story; and (3) each student should select certain words to emphasize orally.

THURS

Objective Interpreting different roles.

Teacher Preparation Provide each student with yellow pages from a telephone book.

Activities Each student selects a business from the yellow pages, and role-plays an employee in that business. The student does not reveal the title of the person portrayed, and other students guess the title. The student should explain orally the services, training, responsibilities, etc., of the employee being role-played.

FRI

Objective Emphasizing vocal key points.

Teacher Preparation Provide each student with a social-studies textbook and a list of words, such as *not, instead of, between, on the other hand, usually, rather than.*

Activities Each group of students selects information from the textbook and writes a sentence that includes a word or phrase from the list. The group performs a choral reading of the sentences, emphasizing the word or phrase and at least one other word in the sentence. Example: Oglethorpe founded *Georgia, not* California.

Notes

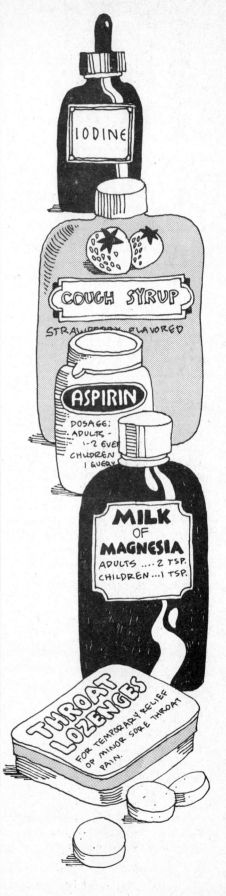

Using Sentences Effectively

18

General Overview Studying how to use different types of sentences should accompany establishment of purposes of various kinds of sentences. During this week, five different types of sentences will be emphasized, each with reference to a different situation and purpose.

Learning Objectives Each student will learn to recognize and interpret the reasons for declarative, directive, interrogative, and exclamatory sentences. In addition, students will expand phrases into sentences.

MON

Objective Reading declarative sentences.

Teacher Preparation Provide each group of students with a newspaper. Briefly explain the concept of declarative sentences.

Activities Each group selects five declarative sentences from the newspaper. Beside each, in newspaper margins, they write a key word or phrase indicating the main idea of the sentence.

TUES

Objective Analyzing medical directives.

Teacher Preparation Bring to class at least ten empty boxes, jars, or vials that had contained medicine and have on them the directions for using. Provide each student with a list of each item.

Activities Students record beside each item the specific directions for using. They also note warning information concerning misuse of the product.

WED

Objective Expanding phrases into sentences.

Teacher Preparation Provide each student with a table of contents in a textbook.

Activities Students refer to the chapters, if necessary, to gather information to use in expanding the chapter title into a sentence. They then write one sentence including each chapter title.

THURS

Objective Reading interrogative sentences.

Teacher Preparation Provide each student with a library book that contains questions in conversations between characters.

Activities Students select five interrogative sentences in the book, and write the page numbers of each, and a key word or phrase indicating the question being asked. Students exchange books and papers. Another student refers to each page indicated and, using the word or phrase guideline, locates the interrogative sentence.

FRI

Objective Reading exclamatory sentences.

Teacher Preparation Provide each student with a comic book.

Activities Each student locates at least one declarative, interrogative, and exclamatory sentence in the comic. The student then draws a line that associates sentence meaning with a segment of the illustration, with emphasis on the exclamatory sentence.

Notes

Improving Handwriting

19

General Overview   In upper-elementary grades and thereafter, the incidence of manuscript writing decreases and cursive writing receives maximum attention. Most people use manuscript only when completing forms and adding emphasis in written communication. Cursive writing, on the other hand, is the major handwriting form used by the majority of people for all other written communication.

Learning Objectives   Each student will practice writing upper- and lower-case forms of both manuscript and cursive handwriting in practical situations.

MON

Objective   Improving upper- and lower-case manuscript letters that are made with predominantly straight lines.

Teacher Preparation   Provide each student with a copy of an order form. Write at least ten different manuscript letters on the chalkboard.

Activities   Students complete in manuscript the items requested on the form (name, address, etc.). They circle manuscript letters indicated on the chalkboard, and "grade" themselves according to the model written by the teacher.

Notes

TUES

Objective   Improving upper- and lower-case manuscript letters that are made with predominantly curved lines.

Teacher Preparation   Provide each student with a copy of an order form (other than the one used on Monday). Write at least twelve manuscript letters on the chalkboard.

Activities   Same as Monday's lesson, except the emphasis is on writing, checking, and improving manuscript letters with predominantly curved lines.

WED

Objective   Improving upper- and lower-case cursive letters that are made with predominantly curved lines.

Teacher Preparation   Write at least eight different cursive letters on the chalkboard.

Activities   Each student writes two telephone memos: (1) a message to another member of the family; and (2) a reminder to self. The student circles in the memos the cursive letters indicated on the chalkboard, compares such letters written against the chalkboard model, and "grades" each.

THURS

Objective   Improving upper- and lower-case cursive letters that are made with predominantly straight lines.

Teacher Preparation   Write on the chalkboard ten items you would like from the grocery store and fifteen different cursive letters.

Activities   Each student writes in cursive at least ten grocery items in a list to be used by someone else on the next trip to the grocery store. The student then circles in the list the cursive letters indicated on the chalkboard, compares his or her handwritten letters with the model on the chalkboard, and assigns a "grade" to each.

FRI

Objective   Recognizing and writing forms of letters other than traditional manuscript or cursive.

Teacher Preparation   Provide each student with a magazine, scissors, paper, and paste.

Activities   Each group of three students develops a poster on a theme decided by that group. They use variant forms of letters found in the magazine, or write other manuscript or cursive letters.

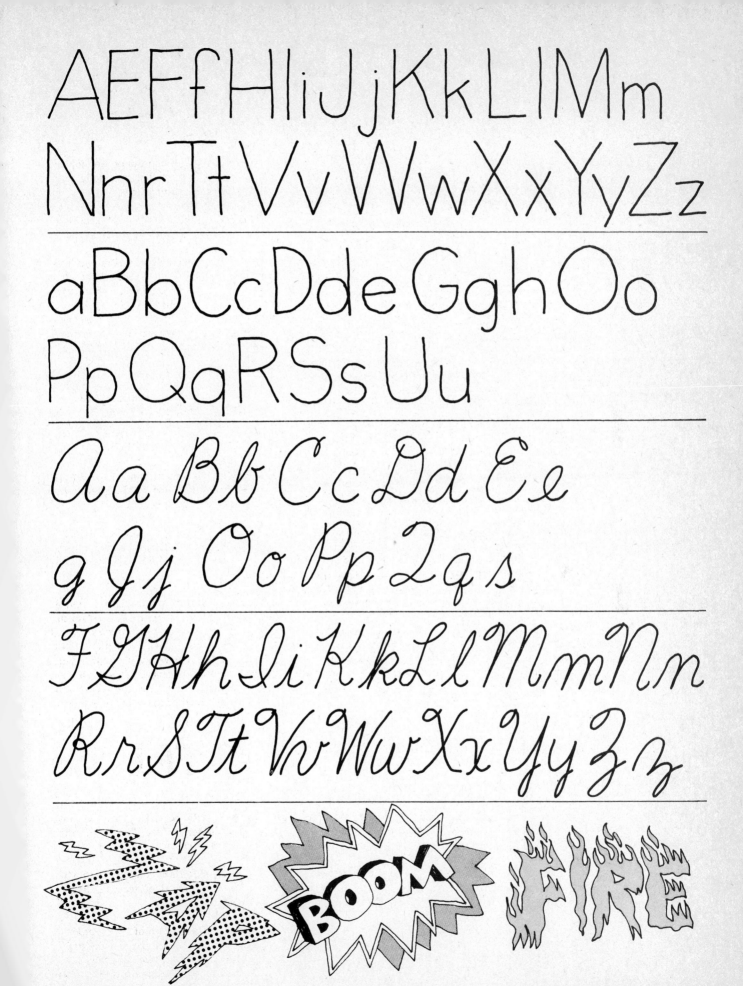

20

General Overview   Asking or receiving information through oral communication is a major communication device, and lessons should be held to assist students in improving these skills. The predominant components in such lessons are: (1) gathering background information; (2) organizing details to communicate; (3) structuring the dissemination of such information; and (4) orally communicating to others.

Learning Objectives   Each student will participate in lessons specifically designed to improve dissemination of information in oral communication. Specific emphasis during the twentieth week is on communicating information about sequence of events, analyzing details, summarizing themes, predicting events, and requesting information.

MON

Objective   Orally noting sequence of events.

Teacher Preparation   Provide each student with an article from the sports section of the newspaper.

Activities   Each student reads the article, places a number beside each event in the story to indicate the sequence of events, and uses the numbers as clues in telling another student the order of events reported.

TUES

Objective   Analyzing detailed information orally.

Teacher Preparation   Provide each student with one page from a catalog.

Activities   The student selects three to five items advertised and notes one detail about each item. The student points to each item selected and reports one detail concerning that item to a partner. Examples:

1. "This hat costs fifteen dollars."
2. "The colors of this coat are blue, white, and green."

WED

Objective   Summarizing global themes orally.

Teacher Preparation   Provide each student with a mathematics textbook.

Activities   Each pair of students selects one subheading in the mathematics textbook and notes at least three main points about that topic. The student then tells another student each point as he/she points to the part of the textbook that indicated the theme to the student.

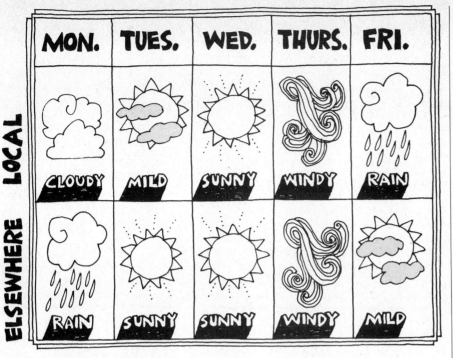

THURS

FRI

Objective Orally asking for specific information.

Teacher Preparation Write items such as *electric lights*, *gas stove*, *sewage*, *water lines*, *telephone* on the chalkboard.

Activities Each student selects one item, composes a question to ask another student about that item, and the two go to the library to locate answers. If answers are not found, they call the utility or telephone company to ask the question.

Objective Predicting events orally.

Teacher Preparation Provide each student with a newspaper weather forecast, paper, and paste, tape, or glue.

Activities Based on information in the weather forecast, each student orally predicts weather for the next day, and any changes that might occur over a week's period both locally and for another section of the country. The student tapes the forecast beside a chart and predicts weather for each day. Refer to the newspaper each day to check prediction.

21

General Overview   Although there is no limit on topics for group discussions, during this week the emphasis is on reasons to study different topics in school. Before Monday a bulletin board should be cleared, and specific space assigned to each *group* of students. After each daily lesson, discussion notes from each group are placed in that space, and different groups can note topical highlights made by other groups. Discussion guidelines that vary from lesson to lesson should be provided each group as one tangible way to help students improve discussion techniques and contributions.

Learning Objectives   Each student will orally contribute to discussions emphasizing reasons students study mathematics, social studies, and science topics in school as well as reasons students are taught spelling and encouraged to improve their handwriting.

MON

Objective   Discussing reasons mathematics is a basic school subject.

Teacher Preparation   Use the following points as a discussion guideline:

1. One way you've used mathematics at home
2. One way your parents use mathematics
3. One way mathematics and money go together

Ask each group to elect a recorder who writes the names of members of the group on a sheet of paper.

Activities   During a time period, each group member discusses the group's guideline item. After time is called, each student writes on the paper beside his/her name one comment made during the discussion. The recorder places the paper on the bulletin board.

TUES

Objective   Discussing reasons spelling is taught in school.

Teacher Preparation   Write these points as a discussion guideline on the chalkboard: (1) *names*, (2) *places*, (3) *things*. The group elects a recorder other than the student who served as recorder on Monday, and the recorder writes the name of each group member on a sheet of paper.

Activities   During a timed period, each group member responds with reasons students learn to spell words for names, places, and tangible items. Each student gives at least one specific example of words under each category. After time is called, follow the procedure described for Monday's lesson.

WED

Objective   Discussing reasons science is a basic school subject.

Teacher Preparation   Have the following discussion guidelines written on the chalkboard:

1. Science at work in the kitchen
2. Evidence of science along a road or sidewalk
3. Science at work in the ceiling of a classroom

Activities   Follow the discussion, recording, and posting of classroom notes described for preceding days in this week.

THURS

Objective   Discussing reasons students are encouraged to improve their handwriting.

Teacher Preparation   Write the following discussion guidelines on the chalkboard:

1. Postal service
2. Business employees
3. Elementary students

Activities   Follow procedure described for Monday's lesson.

FRI

Objective   Discussing reasons social studies is taught in school.

Teacher Preparation   Write the following discussion guidelines on the chalkboard:

1. History of the school
2. Results of politics reported in the newspaper
3. Responsibilities of each family member

Activities   Follow procedure described for Monday's lesson.

22

General Overview The number of forms a person elects or is requested to complete during a lifetime is much larger than even a decade ago. An essential language-arts skill that should be developed, even at the elementary level, is how to correctly complete forms. In addition to the writing tasks, the students need to know the meaning of words such as *residence, zip code, occupation,* etc.

Learning Objectives Each student will read printed information contained on a variety of forms, and write appropriate requested information. The emphasis is on simple academic "work contracts," social-security forms, magazine and newspaper subscriptions, catalog order blanks, and other types of advertisement forms.

MON

Objective Reading and writing class "work contracts."

Teacher Preparation Briefly explain the meaning of a "work contract." Provide each student with a contract form.

Activities Each student selects one content-area textbook, a specific set of assigned work, and completes the contract form by a date selected by the student.

TUES

Objective Completing the application form for a social-security card.

Teacher Preparation Provide each student with a copy of a social-security application card. Briefly discuss selected concepts of social security and the meaning of key words on the application part of the form.

Activities Each student completes the form, and takes it home to discuss with parents whether they wish it mailed.

WED

Objective Completing magazine and/or newspaper subscription forms.

Teacher Preparation Provide each student with a copy of one magazine and one newspaper. Show students where the annual subscription rate and mailing address for subscriptions are found in both the magazine and the newspaper.

Activities Each student writes a letter and addresses a mock envelope placing a hypothetical order for a six-month subscription to either the magazine or newspaper.

THURS

23

Objective Writing an order for one item by using a catalog order form.

Teacher Preparation Provide each student with a copy of an order form from a large catalog firm. Discuss the key places on the form where a person should provide information.

Activities Each student places a small *x* beside each part of the form that should be completed as the teacher cites that part. The student selects one item in the catalog and completes the form to order that item, including taxes and postage.

General Overview The majority of oral reading performed by persons outside a school setting are short and primarily refer to dissemination of specific information. Only in rare instances do people perform extended oral reading to an audience. During the school year, lessons should be held to help students improve short-term oral readings.

Learning Objectives Each student will read orally to other students information frequently associated with oral communication. Such readings include: advertised products, business information, poetic references, and quotations.

FRI

Objective Completing information on order forms found in magazines.

Teacher Preparation Provide each student with scissors, a magazine that contains "fill-in-the-blank" type order information for some of the advertised products, and paste, tape, or glue.

Activities Each student cuts three order forms from the magazine and tapes them on a sheet of paper. The student writes the information requested on each form and compares kinds of information requested.

MON

Objective Oral reading of products and prices advertised as special purchases.

Teacher Preparation Provide each student with a newspaper.

Activities Each student selects one sale advertisement and prepares a thirty-second oral reading composed of noting items in the ad and adding personal comments indicating why the sale price is or is not a good buy.

TUES

Objective Reading orally the name, telephone number, and address of selected businesses.

Teacher Preparation Provide each student with at least three yellow pages from the telephone book.

Activities Each student selects two businesses in the yellow pages, and orally reads, very carefully and with precision, the names, addresses, and telephone numbers of the businesses while another student takes notes.

Notes

WED

Objective Orally reading selected poetic phrases.

Teacher Preparation Provide each student with an action poem. (Example: *Casey at the Bat.*)

Activities Each student selects and silently reads one stanza from the poem before orally reading the stanza. The emphasis is on selecting appropriate vocal expressions to correspond with meanings in the stanza. (*Note:* The same stanza should not be read twice.)

THURS

Objective Selecting and orally reading quotations from newspapers.

Teacher Preparation Ask each student to select one newspaper article containing quotations from at least three different people.

Activities Students in groups of three each select one person quoted in the article, underline statements made by that person, and orally read the quote(s), emphasizing key words spoken.

FRI

Objective Orally interpreting statements made by characters in a book.

Teacher Preparation Provide each student with a novel containing direct quotations of the characters.

Activities Each student in groups of three students reads one quote, using vocal expression that might have been made by the character at different ages, such as a six-year-old, a twenty-year-old, and an eighty-year-old.

General Overview A concern expressed by many teachers is: "But students don't listen!" Scheduling lessons intended to help students improve listening skills is imperative in an elementary language-arts program. In addition to selecting different kinds of situations involving oral communication, definite purposes for listening should be established by the teacher and students.

Learning Objectives Each student will listen and respond to information from a variety of stations and for different reasons. Specifically, students will listen to news information, propaganda, academic information, announcements, and supporting information to general themes.

MON

Objective Listening to current-events information.

Teacher Preparation Provide each student with a current newspaper or news magazine.

Activities Each student selects one article and underlines only words or phrases that contain the base information in the article. The student orally relates the information while other students take notes.

TUES

Objective Listening to propaganda.

Teacher Preparation Bring a transistor radio to class. Turn up the volume so all students can hear when a commercial is broadcast. Write the following listening guides on the chalkboard.

1. Name of product
2. One way it's used
3. Words spoken to try to sell the product

Activities Each student (1) listens to the commerical and (2) notes information contained in the commercial as requested in the listening guide.

WED

Objective Listening for key words to use in note-taking.

Teacher Preparation Give a three-minute lecture on one content-area topic. During the lecture, vocally emphasize at least three words.

Activities Students listen to the lecture and after hearing each word emphasized, they write that word. The class discusses the meaning of the words and how they relate to the lesson theme.

THURS

Objective Listening for support information to main ideas.

Teacher Preparation Provide each student with a science or social-studies textbook.

Activities Each pair of students selects one chapter subheading section. Depending on information in that section, they locate supporting details for each of the following: one *who*, one *where*, one *when*, and one *what*. Other students turn to the page from which the information was taken and the pair of students tell items noted. Other students use that information to locate the paragraphs in which information is found.

FRI

Objective Listening to major items in announcements.

Teacher Preparation Invite the principal to come to the class and make at least three announcements. Place these words on the chalkboard with a blank space following each one: *what, when, who, where,* and *why.*

Activities Students listen to each announcement and the principal provides time for the students to complete information for each category on the chalkboard before giving the next announcement. The principal reviews information from the three announcements using the guide on the chalkboard, and students check to see if they included all pertinent items.

Notes

25

General Overview Accuracy and adequacy are the two major components of reporting, and students need assistance in improving their techniques of disseminating information. Teachers should plan lessons and corresponding assignments to balance oral reports and written reports.

Learning Objectives Each student will prepare and deliver oral and written reports. Specifically, students will make collections of printed materials related to self-selected topics, prepare written reports pertaining to selected changes in a social-studies topic and processes in science, and deliver oral reports emphasizing current events and directions.

MON

Objective Collecting and posting display materials pertaining to one topic.

Teacher Preparation Place strips on the bulletin board so each student in class has one space. Write the student's name on a card and place in the block. One block should contain the teacher's name. Provide each student with magazines, newspapers, and catalogs.

Activities Each student and the teacher select one topic and note the topic on the name card. Each person cuts words, pictures, articles, etc., that pertain to that topic, assembles material, and displays the information in the block. On each item placed on the bulletin board, the person adds at least one word to interpret or explain how that item relates to the topic.

TUES

Objective Writing reports indicating changes in a social-studies topic.

Teacher Preparation Provide students with the social-studies textbook.

Activities Students select one textbook illustration of a person or place. Using information from the textbook as well as from other sources, the students prepare a written report describing changes that have taken place related to that person or place.

WED

Objective Writing reports indicating essential elements in a scientific process.

Teacher Preparation Provide each student with a science textbook. If necessary, show students at least two parts in the textbook where a process is described.

Activities Each student selects one process and lists a chronological sequence of events containing key words from each step in the process. In a block at the bottom of the page, the student writes what is supposed to happen if the steps are followed correctly.

THURS

Objective Making oral reports containing specific directions.

Teacher Preparation Write this list of topics on the chalkboard: *make a game, fly a kite, make jello, build a box, feed a pet, study, ride in a car, ride a bicycle.* Give each student a sheet of paper containing spaces for giving directions.

Activities Each student selects one topic and uses the sequence sheet to note major steps pertaining to the topic. Each student delivers a two-minute talk on the topic. The teacher advises the student when one minute remains.

26

General Overview Lessons emphasizing locating or placing items in alphabetical order should pertain to materials the students will encounter in life situations. In each instance, the initial part of the lesson should pertain to alphabetizing based on the first letter of a word; during subsequent parts of the lesson, students should concentrate on alphabetizing according to the first two, three, and perhaps four letters in words.

Learning Objectives Each student will locate and place in alphabetical order last names of classmates and items found in index entries, telephone books, library card catalogs, and selected stock listings in the newspaper.

FRI

Objective Making oral reports on current events.

Teacher Preparation Provide each student with a recent issue of a newspaper.

Activities Each student selects one news topic, writes major words and phrases from the article on a sheet of paper, and uses these items as guides when delivering an oral report on the topic. The report should be limited to one minute, and the teacher should advise the student when thirty seconds remain.

Notes

MON

Objective Alphabetizing last names of classmates.

Teacher Preparation Provide each student with an unalphabetized list of names of each class member. On the sheet, there should be four columns: *A–F, G–L, M–R,* and *S–Z.*

Activities Each student places the names of classmates in the appropriate column depending on the first letter in the last name.

TUES

Objective Locating selected entries alphabetized in an index.

Teacher Preparation Provide each pair of students with an index taken from a consumable material, such as a catalog, magazine, or road map. Give each student a sheet of paper containing columns for *A–I, J–R,* and *S–Z.*

Activities During this activity, each pair of students should use three different indexes—one for each column. For each index, the students select one topic, and write guide words and page-number references beginning with letters at the top of the column and related to the topic indicated.

A-F G-L M-R S-Z

WED

Objective Locating and alphabetizing information in a telephone book.

Teacher Preparation Provide each pair of students with at least six name entries from the white pages of the telephone book. The first two letters in each entry should be the same, but te rest of the letters unalphabetized (e.g., Thompson, Thomas).

Activities The students determine correct alphabetical order for each name and place that number in front of the item. They cut the items apart and paste them in correct alphabetical order.

THURS

Objective Locating, through the use of alphabetizing, books in the library card catalog.

Teacher Preparation Give each student a three-by-five-inch card containing a topic. Examples of topics are: *horse, zoo, nurse, mystery, vegetable.* Ask students for additional topics.

Activities Each student selects two letters of the alphabet and searches the library card catalog for the names of two books. The author's last name should begin with a letter selected and the topic of the book should be one of those suggested above by the teacher or a student.

FRI

Objective Using alphabetizing skills to locate certain stock listings.

Teacher Preparation Provide each student with a copy of the stock-market quotations in a newspaper. Write these names and any market abbreviations on the chalkboard: Texaco, McDonald's, Shell Oil.

Activities Students use alphabetizing skills to locate on the market page each item listed on the board. They write the item and the closing cost quoted.

Notes

206

General Overview   During this week the teacher should read an adult novel in class for at least ten minutes *each day* while each student reads a library book (or looks at pictures in books if unable to read) selected by that student. No one should be interrupted during this time, and a sign "Read-In—Do Not Disturb" should be taped on the outside of the class door. The lessons in this week are designed to promote the idea that teachers like to read for fun and that recreational reading is important. No student should be asked to report on information read. Following the ten-minute "read-in," time should be provided for least one other type of recreational reading. (Note: The "read-in" is recommended for each remaining day in the year.)

Learning Objectives   Each student will receive time to read for enjoyment in a variety of materials, including library books, comics, horoscopes, record books, joke books, and magazines.

MON

Objective   Starting the "read-in" and reading comics in the classroom.

Teacher Preparation   Each student and teacher should have a library book. Each student also selects a comic book. Tell the students there will be no oral or written questions covering their reading.

Activities   For the first ten minutes of this lesson, students read their library books. Then they are given additional reading time, and the students decide whether they wish to (1) read comics or (2) continue reading their library books.

TUES

Objective   Continuing the "read-in" and reading one's horoscope for the day.

Teacher Preparation   Each person has a library book. Place today's newspaper horoscope on the wall beside the outside door.

Activities   Teacher and students read from the fiction or nonfiction library book for ten minutes. Students read horoscope entries at any time during the school day.

WED

Objective   Continuing the "read-in" and finding items of interest in a records book such as *Guinness Book of World Records*.

Teacher Preparation   Each person has a library book. Have multiple copies of books such as the Guinness book in the classroom.

Activities   All read from a library book for ten minutes. Each student then selects one topic of interest and, sometime during the school day, looks in the records book to locate unusual information about that topic.

THURS

28

Objective Continuing the "read-in" and reading jokes and/or riddles.

Teacher Preparation Each person has a library book. Have in the classroom copies of joke and/or riddle books, and individual jokes pasted on paper.

Activities Each person reads from the library book for ten minutes. The person then decides whether to (1) continue reading the library book or (2) read jokes and/or riddles.

General Overview At least one reading skill should be identified and emphasized within *each* content-area lesson. As a result, reading lessons are not isolated from reading within academic subjects. During the twenty-eighth week, one reading skill is suggested for inclusion in a content-area lesson. The lesson topics indicated are for illustration only, and the teacher should substitute appropriate content-area topics for each day.

Learning Objectives Each student will improve one specific reading skill in the following content areas: mathematics, physical science, history, geography, and English grammar.

FRI

Objective Continuing the "read-in" and reading items of interest in a popular magazine.

Teacher Preparation Each person has a library or trade book. Let each student also select a magazine.

Activities Each person in the classroom reads from a library book for ten minutes and then decides whether to (1) read from the magazine or (2) continue reading the library book.

Notes

MON

Objective Reading mathematics formulas.

Teacher Preparation Write on the chalkboard four different formulas from the mathematics textbook. Beside each item in the first formula, show the student where the meaning of that item is discussed in the textbook; draw a line from the formula item and write the meaning of the symbol at the end of the line.

Activities Each student at his/her desk follows the procedure in identifying from the textbook and noting on paper the words that describe each part of the remaining formulas.

THE MOON ORBITS THE EARTH AT A MEAN DISTANCE OF 238,857 MILES AND HAS A DIAMETER OF 2,160 MILES.

TUES

Objective Associating information in captions with physical-science textbook illustrations.

Teacher Preparation Provide each student with page references to three illustrations with captions from the science textbook.

Activities Each student reads the captions and lists each word in the caption that has a meaning illustrated.

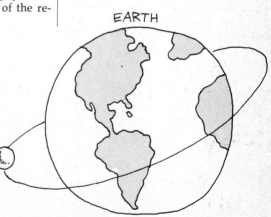

EARTH

WED

Objective Identifying and associating selected people and events in a history lesson.

Teacher Preparation Ask each student to locate one paragraph in a history textbook that contains references to at least two people.

Activities The student writes the name of each person, and beside the name notes an accomplishment as described in the textbook.

THURS

Objective Locating and reading specific map points in a geography lesson.

Teacher Preparation Ask each pair of students to turn to a physical map in a geography or history textbook.

Activities Using only information in the map, the students note information with reference to the following topics: (1) the best place to take a vacation; (2) "trouble spots" on the map; (3) the largest single land area; (4) the largest water area.

FRI

Objective Noting the effect of verb tense in an English grammar lesson.

Teacher Preparation Provide each group of students with at least one page reference to a grammar lesson on verb tense in the English textbook and magazines.

Activities One student in each group writes at the top of a page a verb tense as found in the grammar lesson. The students locate magazine pictures or words that place the verb in past, present, and future tense. Repeat the procedure for other verbs.

Notes

44

Writing Creatively

General Overview Encouraging each student to combine words in unique and individualized ways to communicate information is the base of creative-writing lessons. For these writings, no grades should be given, and no spelling or grammar errors should be marked by the teacher. The objective is to find various ways in which to motivate students to express themselves through writing.

Learning Objectives Each student will produce a creative writing based on the following: one selected word, a picture, a book or record jacket, an emotion, and television characters.

MON

Objective Writing creatively to expand interpretations given to a particular word.

Teacher Preparation Ask each student to open a book, point to one word, and center that word on the first line of a sheet of paper. *Only* after the word is written does the teacher ask each student to write a story with the word as a subject. (*Note:* Words such as *and, the, because,* as well as *apple* have been the topics of creative stories written by students.)

Activities Each student writes until time is called (no more than five minutes), then exchanges paper with another student. Each adds to the story written by the partner.

TUES

Objective Interpreting picture scenes through creative writing.

Teacher Preparation Provide each student with a magazine from which the student selects one picture. Place these guidelines on the chalkboard: *who, what, when, where, how,* and *why.*

Activities Each student writes a story related to the picture theme, including specific information with reference to each guide word written on the chalkboard.

WED

Objective Expanding thoughts through creative writing concerning the contents of a book or record jacket.

Teacher Preparation Provide each student with a book or record jacket. Write on the chalkboard "The Life of This Book/Record Jacket."

Activities Each student selects the appropriate title from the chalkboard and writes a creative interpretation of the life of the item to include: infancy, teenage, adulthood.

THURS

Objective Creating a written scene to include effects of different emotions.

Teacher Preparation Provide each student with a comic book. Help students identify character expression of emotions, such as happiness, sadness, fear, anger, frustration, etc.

Activities Each student writes a story or poem concerning one comic character and the reasons that character might experience at least four different emotions.

FRI

Objective Writing a plot to depict the actions and/or thoughts of television characters from different programs.

Teacher Preparation Lead a discussion of the students' favorite television programs and the roles played by major characters. Write on the chalkboard the names of the characters and a name for each role.

Activities Each student selects two characters from *two* different television programs and writes a plot including both characters.

Notes

Improving Speech Sounds

30

General Overview Improvement in enunciation of speech sounds is basic to more effective oral communication. Most people, especially those with speech handicaps, can benefit from lessons emphasizing formation of speech sounds.

Learning Objectives Each student will isolate and pronounce consonant sounds, with concentrated emphasis on specific voicing of the sound.

MON

Objective Making the s sound.

Teacher Preparation Identify five items in the class that begin with s. Emphasize the initial sound and ask students to repeat the words. Provide each pair of students with grocery advertisements from the newspaper.

Activities Students in each pair take turns pronouncing items that begin with s, and adding the plural sound of s to items that can have that sound. (Examples: sugar; shrimp; strawberry—strawberries.)

TUES

Objective Making the r sound.

Teacher Preparation Provide each pair of students with a section from the white pages of the telephone book where the r listings are found. Pronounce the r sound with the students.

Activities Each student takes turns pronouncing last names that begin with r and any first names that contain r.

WED

Objective Making the w sound.

Teacher Preparation Show each pair of students how to find the w section in a textbook index. Pronounce with the students the sound of w.

Activities Each student takes turns pronouncing each item that begins with w as well as other words in that section that contain w.

THURS

Objective Making the l sound.

Teacher Preparation As each student pronounces the l sound, hold a mirror before the student so he or she can see the tip of the tongue touch the roof of the mouth. Pronounce with the students the l sound.

Activities Each student writes at least three mock newspaper headlines, each containing as many words that begin with or include the sound of l. As each student reads the headlines, other students note the number of times l is heard.

FRI

Objective Selecting and voicing other consonant sounds.

Teacher Preparation Ask each pair of students to locate a sentence containing at least ten words.

Activities The students isolate and pronounce each consonant sound found in each word in the sentence. They discuss which consonants have voiced sounds, and which do not.

Notes

Locating Causes and Effects

31

General Overview The ability to note causes and consequences of personal ideas and actions as well as objects and events in society has a direct application to daily living. The major focus of this lesson is on recognition of kinds of causes and effects and the various degrees of responses made by people.

Learning Objectives Each student will identify causes and effects of selected occupations, transportation devices, machinery, current events, and personal duties.

MON

Objective Detecting causes and effects of selected jobs.

Teacher Preparation Lead students in a brief discussion of the reasons for and effects of various occupations. Those recommended for today's lesson are jobs related to aspects of housing, education, health, and business.

Activities Each small group of students selects two occupation categories and for each notes three reasons such a job exists and three effects on others as a result of work done in the occupation. Specific job titles within the categories also should be discussed.

TUES

Objective Identifying causes and effects of various kinds of transportation.

Teacher Preparation Provide each pair of students with a magazine and a history textbook.

Activities Students make a list of each type of transportation found in magazine and textbook pictures. Each group of students discusses two causes and two effects of each type of transportation.

WED

Objective Discussing causes and effects of different machines.

Teacher Preparation Provide each group of three students with a catalog containing machines and machine parts.

Activities Each group selects references to three different machines and notes the parts list. They select one part for each machine and discuss one reason the part is needed or added to the machine as an optional item, and one effect on the use of the machine if the part is broken or not purchased.

THURS

Objective Discerning causes and effects in current events.

Teacher Preparation Provide each student with a news article from the front page of a newspaper or a lead story in a news magazine.

Activities The student draws one line under each cause identified in the article, and draws two lines under each effect noted. Students discuss whether the headline or story title describes a cause, an effect, or a combination of both cause and effect.

FRI

Objective Noting causes and effects of personal actions.

Teacher Preparation Ask each student to identify three typical actions made by that student during a day. Examples: eating breakfast, watching television, making bed, etc.

Activities For each action, the student notes four reasons or causes of the action, and two effects when the action is taken. The student notes one possible effect if, for example, breakfast is skipped.

Notes

Detecting Facts and Opinions

32

General Overview Unfortunately, the majority of students believe "If it's in print, it's true." To offset this erroneous assumption, lessons should be directed at helping students to differentiate between specific facts that are indisputable as opposed to opinions or value judgments related to the facts.

Learning Objectives Each student will locate facts and opinions written in advertisements, editorials, descriptions of characters, news articles, and travel brochures.

MON

Objective Locating facts and opinions in advertisements.

Teacher Preparation Provide each pair of students with one full-page advertisement in a magazine and a sheet of paper with two columns headed: *100% True* and *Not 100% True.*

Activities Each pair of students notes in the first column words, phrases, or sentences in the advertisement that are true and cannot be disputed. In the second column, the students write words that do not convey the whole truth or could be misleading.

TUES

Objective Separating words that represent facts from words reflecting opinions in editorials.

Teacher Preparation Provide each group of three students with a newspaper editorial.

Activities Students circle all words in the editorial that are value judgments and have been placed in the editorial to present a point of view.

WED

Objective Locating words that reflect value judgments in descriptions of characters and historical figures.

Teacher Preparation Provide each student with a social-studies textbook and a library book containing stories involving different characters.

Activities In each book, the students locate descriptive words for at least three historical figures or characters. They categorize each word selected that would describe a thing liked and a thing disliked, depending on their interpretation of the descriptive words.

UGLY

FAST

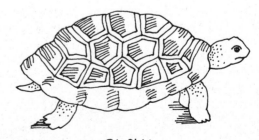

SLOW

THURS

FRI

Objective Locating facts and opinions in news articles.

Teacher Preparation Provide each student with a news story from a newspaper.

Activities The student draws one line under each phrase or sentence in the news article that is a fact. Two lines should be drawn under any items in the article that reflect an interpretation of the facts, or an opinion concerning the facts.

Objective Identifying facts versus biased interpretation of facts in travel brochures.

Teacher Preparation Provide each pair of students with a travel brochure or ask students to locate a travel advertisement in a magazine.

Activities The students make a poster by centering facts in the advertisement in the middle of the poster, and placing words, phrases, or sentences that represent "incentives" to visit the places on lines extending from the facts.

Locating Supporting Details

33

General Overview   The ability to locate pertinent supporting details and to screen out irrelevant information is a basic language-arts skill that should be improved during the elementary years. In each lesson during the thirty-third week, the emphasis is on distinguishing between primary supporting details and information that might be considered "padding."

Learning Objectives   Each student will identify and contrast major supporting details with material that could have been omitted without distorting the subject.

MON

Objective   Locating supporting details and excess materials in a diagram or chart.

Teacher Preparation   Provide each pair of students with a diagram or chart.

Activities   Students identify three facts in the diagram or chart that are essential to the chart theme, and one item that is not as important to the theme. Discuss reasons for the selection of both types of information.

TUES

Objective   Locating basic information and less relevant "sell" information in business advertisements in a telephone directory.

Teacher Preparation   Provide each student with pages from the yellow pages of a telephone book.

Activities   Each student pastes one block advertisement in the center of a sheet of paper. Beneath the advertisement, the student writes words or phrases in the advertisement that are essential information to a prospective customer. Above the advertisement, the student notes words, phrases, and/or illustrations containing information that is not as essential.

WED

Objective   Identifying essential supporting details in mathematics "word" problems.

Teacher Preparation   Provide each student with at least two "word" problems from the mathematics textbook.

Activities   Each student makes a list of the essential numerals, words, and phrases necessary to work the problem. The student counts the number of words or numerals that could have been omitted in the problem.

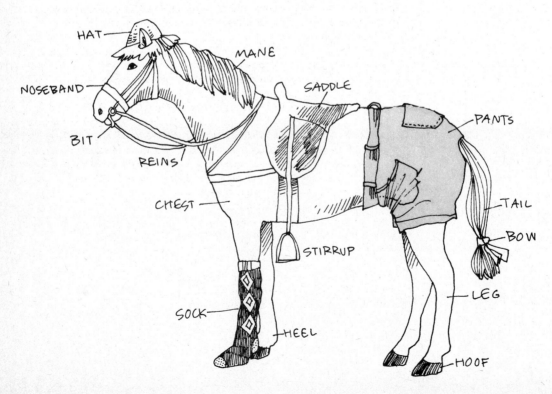

THURS

Objective Noting basic support information in catalog descriptions of items for sale.

Teacher Preparation Provide each student with one page containing several items for sale in a catalog.

Activities The student circles each part of the catalog descriptions that a person needs to know before making a choice of which item to purchase from that page.

FRI

Objective Identifying critical supporting details to a theme in an academic-area textbook.

Teacher Preparation Provide each group of students with a page reference to a subheading in a textbook.

Activities The group reads the subheadings, and all members of the group locate details that relate directly to that subheading. Class discussion should be held concerning that information.

Notes

34

General Overview The process of selecting appropriate verbs to correspond with intended communication concerning an action and selecting descriptive adverbs to further enhance communication should not be separated. Instead, lessons should help students learn to associate adverbs with verbs and to select the most appropriate of each. During the thirty-fourth week, each lesson contains references to the newspaper, but other types of printed material could be substituted.

On Monday, place on the bulletin board a sheet for each student containing the emphasis topic for each day of the week. For Monday, the topic is *advice;* for Tuesday, *sports;* for Wednesday, *titles;* for Thursday, *society;* for Friday, *creative writing.* At the conclusion of each day's lesson, Monday through Friday, the student lists verbs and adverbs that he or she has located or selected during the lesson.

Learning Objectives Each student will learn to locate verbs used to refer to specific categories of information, and to locate in print or from other sources adverbs that clarify the verbs.

MON

Objective Locating verbs and adverbs in the Dear Abby/Ann Landers type of newspaper column.

Teacher Preparation Tape or paste one letter to Ann or Abby on the front of a three-by-five-inch card; put the response to the letter on the back of the same card.

Activities The student circles each verb in the letter and underlines any adverbs describing the verbs. On a separate sheet, before reading the response, the student writes a response to the letter, using the same verbs and different adverbs. For each verb or verb phrase, the student must write a descriptive adverb. The student then reads the printed response on the back of the card and compares that information with the student's recommendations. The student completes the first column on the sheet on the bulletin board.

TUES

Objective Selecting verbs and adverbs related to sports topics.

Teacher Preparaion Provide each student with articles from the sports section of the newspaper.

Activities Each student circles each verb and underlines each adverb found in at least two sports articles. If no adverb is written, the student inserts an adverb for each verb. Write the verbs and adverbs in the second column on the bulletin board.

WED

Objective Relating headline verbs and adverbs.

Teacher Preparation Provide each student with at least five headlines from front pages of newspapers.

Activities The student circles the verbs in the headlines and unless an adverb is in the headline, inserts an adverb that describes the verb. The student writes these verbs and adverbs in the third column on the bulletin board.

THURS

Objective Locating verbs and adverbs related to society news.

Teacher Preparation Provide each student with at least two items from the society section of the newspaper.

Activities The student follows the activities procedure described for Wednesday, selecting and writing verbs and adverbs from the society articles. The student writes these verbs and adverbs in the fourth column on the page on the bulletin board.

FRI

Objective Comparing the different categories of verbs and adverbs and incorporating selected verbs and adverbs in a creative writing.

Teacher Preparation Provide each student with the sheet of verbs and adverbs written during the week.

Activities Each student writes a story or poem using as many of the verbs and adverbs on the sheet as possible. Each time one is used in the writing, the student places an *x* beside the word on the sheet.

MON.		TUES.		WED.		THURS.		FRI.	
ADVICE		SPORTS		TITLES		SOCIETY		CREATIVE WRITING	
V.	ADV.	V.	ADV.	V.	ADV.	V.	ADV.	V.	ADV.
listen	carefully	jump	high	reacts	promptly	speak	cheerfully	arrived	late

Notes

Improving Reactions to Various Punctuation Marks

35

General Overview Students need to learn to associate different punctuation marks with appropriate responses in (1) selecting and writing the correct punctuation mark, and (2) adjusting reading rate or vocal expression to the influence of a punctuation mark. In each lesson during the thirty-fifth week, the teacher should emphasize the punctuation mark in both reading and writing.

Learning Objectives Each student will respond in oral interpretation and in written use to the following punctuation marks: question marks, periods, quotation marks, commas, and dashes.

MON

Objective Using and reacting to question marks.

Teacher Preparation Provide each pair of students with a textbook containing word or phrase subheadings in chapters, and a comic book.

Activities (1) *Using questions:* Each student orally converts a textbook subheading into a question and reads the subheading material to locate answers to the question. (2) *Reacting to question marks:* Students in pairs take turns locating questions in the comic book and reading the question to the partner. Oral emphasis is on voice inflections denoting questioning.

WED

Objective Using and reacting to quotation marks.

Teacher Preparation Provide each student with a library book containing quotations.

Activities (1) *Using quotation marks:* Each student circles at least four quotations found in library books. One student reads the part wherein the speaker is identified; the other student reads the direct quotation. (2) *Reacting to quotation marks:* One student makes a short oral statement; the partner writes the words in quotation marks and adds explanatory material outside the quotation marks.

FRI

Objective Using and reacting to dashes.

Teacher Preparation Discuss various ways dashes are used.

Activities (1) *Using dashes:* After the discussion, each student writes one paragraph, including in the paragraph a set of dashes. (2) *Reacting to dashes:* Student locates pages in an English grammar textbook and discusses the reason for each example of the use of dashes.

Notes

TUES

Objective Using and reacting to periods.

Teacher Preparation Provide each pair of students with a newspaper and a science textbook.

Activities (1) *Using periods:* Each student writes at least three declarative sentences or adds words to newspaper headlines to convert the headlines into declarative sentences. (2) *Reacting to periods:* Each pair of students selects at least three declarative sentences from the science textbook and reads the sentences aloud, orally placing emphasis on key words in the sentences.

THURS

Objective Using and reacting to commas.

Teacher Preparation Provide each student with sections from the "Pets for Sale" or "Automobiles for Sale" newspaper classified advertisements.

Activities (1) *Using commas:* Each student writes at least two sentences, each containing items separated by commas. Examples:

The least expensive pets are ___, ___, and ___.

The oldest automobiles for sale are ___, ___, and ___.

(2) *Reacting to commas:* The students read the sentences with pauses to indicate each comma.

Learning to Enjoy Poetry

36

General Overview Helping students enjoy reading poetry depends on (1) the teacher's enthusiasm and explanation of poetry; (2) many volumes of poetry in the classroom (at least one collection of poems per student); (3) no required memorizing of poems; (4) no required copying of poems; and (5) an emphasis on self-selection and personal interpretation of poems. Each student should be encouraged to locate poems in different poetry books during this week, with the teacher providing categorical guidelines for selecting poems to read. Small group discussions of the poem should be a part of each lesson.

Learning Objectives Each student will select and read a variety of poems in the following categories: people, animals, events, nature, and achievements.

MON

Objective Interpreting poems about people.

Teacher Preparation Provide each student with a collection of poems and a magazine.

Activities Each student locates at least one poem about a person, reads the poem, and discusses references to the person with another student. The student selects magazine pictures of people that can be associated with the person in the poem, pastes the pictures on a sheet of paper, and writes descriptive words from the poem around the pictures.

TUES

Objective Interpreting poems about animals.

Teacher Preparation Provide each student with a collection of poems. The book should not be the same as the one read on Monday.

Activities Each student locates and reads at least one poem about an animal and discusses the poem with another student. Each student then selects one animal and writes a poem about that animal.

WED

Objective Reading poems describing events.

Teacher Preparation Provide each student with a different book of poems from the books read on Monday and Tuesday.

Activities Each student reads at least one poem concerning an event and discusses the poem with another student. The major guideline for discussion is: in the poem, which is the most important—the event itself or the result of the event?

"Under a spreading chestnut-tree"

"Quoth the raven, 'Nevermore!'"

THURS

FRI

Objective Interpreting poems about nature.

Teacher Preparation Provide each student with a collection of poems that the student has not seen this week.

Activities Each student selects at least one poem describing some aspect of nature and discusses with another student the words used in the poem to describe natural events. The students discuss the effect of these words on the meanings in the poems.

Objective Reading poems depicting achievements.

Teacher Preparation Provide each student with a different collection of poems from the ones read earlier in the week.

Activities Each student selects at least one poem concerning an achievement made by a person. Small group discussions are held to discuss the various achievements noted and how the poems tell the stories. Each student then writes one poem describing a personal achievement made in school during this academic year.

"On the shores of Gitche Gumee"

Social Studies

Social Studies

1 Emphasizing the Value of Self	**2** Emphasizing the Value of Education	**3** Recognizing Contributions of Family Members
4 Discerning Various Aspects of Vacation Traveling	**5** Learning Different Address Forms	**6** Learning Contributions of Public Service
7 Noting Different Aspects of Housing	**8** Learning Ways to Budget Money	**9** Studying about Ecology
10 Learning about Different Forms of Machine-Based Transportation	**11** Discerning Different Uses of Leisure Time	**12** Discovering Contributions of Sports to Society
13 Comparing Different Foods	**14** Learning to Read Maps	**15** Studying Career Education
16 Learning Contributions of Different Ethnic Groups	**17** Deemphasizing Sex-Role Stereotypes	**18** Developing the Concept of Patriotism

19

Detecting Reasons for Conflicts

20

Learning about Clothing

21

Recognizing Various Kinds
of Freedoms

22

Recognizing Major Purposes
of Selected Institutions

23

Noting Elements in
Group Process

24

Assuming Responsibilities

25

Learning Various
Governmental Operations

26

Locating Selected
Current Events

27

Learning through Television

28

Learning Aspects of History of
Different Ethnic Groups

29

Recognizing Contributions of
Females and Males

30

Learning about Selected
Major Dates

31

Detecting Propaganda

32

Learning Contributions of
Selected Occupations

33

Detecting Messages

34

Learning Why Selected Places
Are Considered Important

35

Studying Another Country

36

Identifying Causes of
Major Events

Emphasizing the Value of Self

General Overview   Attention should be given at all times to the value of each student as an important person in society with ideas and actions that contribute to individual and group efforts. This emphasis should be initiated during the first week in lessons such as those below. Each student is important and, in his or her own way, has much to offer others. One role of the teacher is to direct the development of this concept in the classroom.

Learning Objectives   During the first week specific learning opportunities will be provided for each student to discern aspects of his or her own contributions to individual and group work and play themes, such as safety, helping others, friendship, and idea formation.

MON

Objective   Associating one's knowledge of safety rules with helping younger children.

Teacher Preparation   Develop a series of five instances in which a person may face possible danger and role-play each example. Examples: (1) standing on a corner watching a traffic light; (2) touching an electrical outlet in the classroom; (3) holding a pencil; (4) standing in an elevator and on an escalator; (5) taking medicine.

Activities   Students observe each role enactment and discuss what each would tell a younger child concerning safety precautions.

TUES

Objective   Identifying a variety of occasions when one person helps another.

Teacher Preparation   Provide each pair of students with a magazine, paper, pencils, and tape or glue.

Activities   Each pair of students locates pictures that indicate some aspects of one person helping another. They tear the pictures from the magazine and paste them on a sheet of paper. They must write at least one word indicating how assistance is being given in each picture.

WED

Objective   Locating specific examples of how students in the class contribute to group efforts.

Teacher Preparation   Give each student a sheet of paper with a topic written at the top. Examples: *Helping at Home; Helping in the Grocery Store; Caring for School Property; Working on a School Project.* Divide the class into groups of three.

Activities   Each group member tells or writes one item he or she could contribute to the topic.

THURS

Objective   Noting different types and degrees of friendship.

Teacher Preparation   Give each pair of students a stencil, such as the example shown, along with newspapers, tape or glue, and pencils.

Activities   Each pair of students writes words or phrases indicating at least one way in which friendship can be shown with reference to each topic. They search in newspaper stories for words they can associate with friendship, and paste those words on the page in the appropriate space.

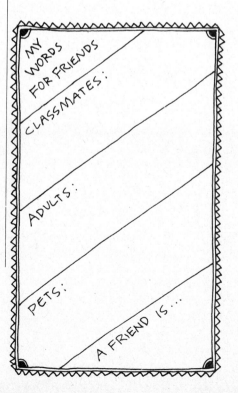

MY WORDS FOR FRIENDS
CLASSMATES:
ADULTS:
PETS:
A FRIEND IS:...

FRI

Objective Assigning positive values to each student's ideas.

Teacher Preparation Write three words on the chalkboard. Examples: *History, Work, People.*

Activities Each student selects any of the three words and tells what he or she thinks about the topic. The teacher accepts each contribution and encourages the student's concept of the importance of his or her ideas by verbally noting a positive statement about what the student said.

Notes

General Overview Rather than deliver a lecture on the values of education, the teacher should encourage students to arrive at conclusions concerning the benefits of educational experiences as a result of analyzing life situations. Topics introduced during this week should be expanded during the remainder of the academic year to include other benefits from education.

Learning Objectives Each student will identify the values of education in teaching people to read, write, and compute. In addition, each student will discuss contributions of education to science and various occupations.

MON

Objective Discovering educational effects of learning to read.

Teacher Preparation Show each of the following to the students and lead a discussion on why people need to be asked to read each and what kinds of basic information people need from the printed materials:

—driver's license manual
—classified advertisement section of the newspaper
—prescription label
—library book
—calendar
—machine manual
—copy of rules and regulations

Activities Each student, in groups of four students, states at least one reason people need to be able to read each of the items identified by the teacher.

TUES

Objective Noting educational effects of learning to write clearly and legibly.

Teacher Preparation Provide each student with an envelope and an order form. Lead a brief discussion concerning what may happen if the handwriting is not specific and legible on both items.

Activities Each student completes in handwriting both the order form and the envelope. In small groups, the students make a list of the people who will read their writing on the items.

WED

Objective Noting educational effects of learning elementary mathematics.

Teacher Preparation Provide each student with a budget form.

Activities Each student completes the form, selecting sums for each item as projected over a one-month period. Additional items on the form are to be supplied by the individual student. The student notes the difference between total income and total expenses. Discuss the importance of adding and subtracting in household and personal budgets.

THURS

Objective Noting effects of education in science-related topics.

Teacher Preparation Place the following list on the chalkboard: *doctor of medicine, carpenter, electrician, taxi driver.*

Activities Each pair of students discusses: (1) what effect science has on persons in the occupations listed, and (2) in what facets of science persons in each occupation must be knowledgeable.

FRI

Objective Detecting effects of education on selected occupations.

Teacher Preparation Provide each student with a magazine.

Activities Each pair of students looks at magazine pictures and article titles to identify people in various kinds of occupations. For each found, the students make a list of items that person must study in order to be successful in the job.

Notes

Recognizing Contributions of Family Members

General Overview The teacher should be extremely careful not to present family members in sex-stereotyped roles. The emphasis is on recognizing contributions of family members rather than on differentiating males from females regarding different kinds of contributions to home and society. No student should be required to identify too closely with his or her own family; for some, the topic may be sensitive as a result of imprisonment of a family member, desertion, or a host of other possible reasons.

Learning Objectives Each student will discuss possible contributions made by family members to home improvement, volunteer work, income-producing work, home-based recreation, and care for others who live in the home.

MON

Objective Noting contributions to home improvement.

Teacher Preparation Provide each pair of students with a copy of a catalog.

Activities Students locate items in the catalog that are basic to home life and home repairs. For each, they discuss:

1. Why is this item used in the home?
2. Which family members usually use the item?
3. Which ones could use it if that person was ill or away from home?
4. What do I need to do to learn to use the item?

TUES

Objective Noting nonpaid services to others.

Teacher Preparation Lead a brief discussion concerning various ways relatives help other members of the family without monetary compensation.

Activities Each student completes the chart by inserting one item that has been accomplished without pay during each time period by: (1) someone else in the family helping the student, and (2) the student helping someone else in the family. The time can refer to any day in the week.

WED

Objective Noting contribution from income-producing work.

Teacher Preparation Avoid asking each student the occupation of his or her parents. Instead, concentrate on the contribution provided to the home as a result of income earned by adults. Lead a discussion on: "What kinds of things does job income purchase for use at home?"

Activities Start a series of blocks on the chalkboard and add items as noted by the students. Use the following to initiate the discussion: *food, kitchen utensils, heating, television set, newspaper.*

THURS

Objective Noting recreation in the home.

Teacher Preparation The emphasis in today's lesson is on discussing different hobbies and other forms of home-based recreation, such as watching television, knitting, carving wood.

Activities Use the procedure described for Wednesday's lesson.

FRI

Objective Noting contributions to basic survival conditions.

Teacher Preparation The theme of today's lesson is based on all able members of the family working together to provide basic living conditions. Begin the discussion with the question: "What must people have at home simply to live?"

Activities Use the format described for Wednesday's lesson. After items have been identified, each student is asked to think through his or her contribution in ensuring the continuation of each item.

Notes

Discerning Various Aspects of Vacation Traveling

General Overview Travel obviously involves more than transportation. Students need to learn that forethought must be given to arranging for basic necessities as well as unexpected emergencies. Before Monday the teacher should have collected enough travel brochures so each student will have access to at least one brochure. Each day during the week, each student uses a brochure that describes a different place. Reference materials containing information about the places described in the brochures should also be in the classroom.

Learning Objectives Each student will analyze factors concerning food, clothing, travel rate schedules, tourist sites, and monetary exchange rates associated with various places to visit.

MON

Objective Learning about different foods in various countries.

Teacher Preparation Provide each student with a travel brochure describing a foreign country and access to recipe books.

Activities Students read the brochure to find out if special foods are mentioned. They locate recipes in the cookbook that have the name of foreign countries in them (Swedish meat balls, French fried potatoes).

TUES

Objective Anticipating clothing needs for different climates.

Teacher Preparation Provide each student with another travel brochure, and access to a clothing catalog.

Activities Students read the brochure for information concerning what kinds of clothing to pack for the trip. Then they select that kind of clothing from the catalog.

WED

Objective Computing expenses for different modes of travel.

Teacher Preparation Provide each small group of students with a travel brochure containing rates by ship and one containing rates by air.

Activities Students analyze the expense difference by air or ship to the places described on the brochures. They note what items are included in the tickets.

THURS

Objective Locating places of interest to visit.

Teacher Preparation Provide each student with a different travel brochure and access to encyclopedias.

Activities Students underline references to vacation spots as described on the brochures. They refer to the encyclopedia to see if information concerning these spots is included and whether the encyclopedia has information concerning the city and country.

FRI

Objective Computing rates of exchange of U.S. dollars with currencies of foreign countries.

Teacher Preparation Obtain a recent currency exchange rate.

Activities Each pair of students makes a budget including items such as hotel, food, tickets to vacation spots, etc., and selects a hypothetical amount of U.S. dollars to take on the trip. Then they use the exchange rate for the selected country to compute the value of the dollar in that country.

Notes

Learning Different Address Forms

5

General Overview   There are many forms of printed and oral address between people. In addition to learning to write postal addresses, students need to recognize commonly used titles and their abbreviations for categories of people. From an oral standpoint, role-playing ways of addressing people should be a part of the social-studies program.

Learning Objectives   Each student will learn to correctly address envelopes, to associate frequently used titles and abbreviations of titles of people, and to improve techniques of introducing oneself on the telephone and in personal encounters.

MON

Objective   Learning to address envelopes.

Teacher Preparation   Provide each student with a copy of the new state abbreviations suggested for use by the U.S. Postal Service, a map of the United States, and at least two envelopes.

Activities   The student writes on each state in the map the new abbreviation for that state. The student addresses one envelope to Mr. _____ and the second envelope to Ms. _____. If possible, the student goes to the post office and uses the zip-code directory as a part of a hypothetical envelope address, incorporating street, city, and state.

TUES

Objective   Associating titles with title abbreviations of politicians.

Teacher Preparation   Provide each student with a copy of a news magazine such as *Newsweek* and *Time*, as well as a newspaper. Place a list of titles and abbreviations on the chalkboard. Examples: Senator (Sen.), President (Pres.).

Activities   Students locate titles of politicians in the magazine or newspaper and write the titles in the first column. In the second column they write the abbreviation. If the abbreviation is found, they write it in the second column and use a dictionary if necessary in spelling the title.

WED

Objective   Associating titles with abbreviations of titles of professional persons.

Teacher Preparation   Provide each small group of students with a telephone book.

Activities   Use the same procedure described for Tuesday's lesson, except the emphasis is on titles and abbreviation of titles of professionals, such as doctors, dentists, attorneys, etc.

THURS

Objective   Learning to make telephone introductions.

Teacher Preparation   Lead a brief discussion covering different kinds of introductory information a person gives over the telephone depending on the nature of the call.

Activities   One student role-plays an employee of a business and another student role-plays a person calling the firm for the first time. For the next hypothetical call to a firm, the students exchange roles. In each instance the "employee" takes notes. Suggested calls are to: (1) a veterinarian because a pet is ill; (2) a florist to wire flowers to a friend; (3) an electrician to repair an oven; and (4) a motel to reserve a room.

FRI

Objective   Addressing others in personal conversations.

Teacher Preparation   Provide each pair of students with a comic book.

Activities   Students select a comic character and read the cartoon conversation as if addressing another character. The emphasis is on adjusting vocal expressions to improve the exchange of information.

Learning Contributions of Public Service

6

General Overview The concept of a part of tax dollars being used to provide public service is an essential aspect in social studies. If possible, before this week, the teacher should gather statistics on the amount of tax monies spent in various public-service categories and include this information in class discussion. Information requested from various city and county public-service departments will be helpful also in this week's lessons.

Learning Objectives Each student will learn to associate a basic relationship between tax support and public services. In addition, the student will study the kinds of public service found in education, transportation, protection of life and property, government, and public records.

MON

Objective Learning about public services in education.

Teacher Preparation List three columns on the chalkboard (*People, Items, Buildings*) and lead a class discussion of items that can be placed in each column.

Activities Students note one reason and public service for each item listed on the chalkboard.

TUES

Objective Learning public services that facilitate transportation.

Teacher Preparation Follow the procedure described for Monday's lesson, except the emphasis in today's lesson is on the use of public funds to improve walking or riding (public transportation stations, roads, sidewalks, public recreation centers).

Activities Students identify one aspect in each place noted that is designed to facilitate safe transportation.

WED

Objective Learning about the various kinds of public health and protection services.

Teacher Preparation Follow the same procedure described for Monday's lesson, except the emphasis is on public health and physical/property protection (police, fire, ambulance, public-health department).

Activities For each item noted, the students identify at least three different kinds of public services offered.

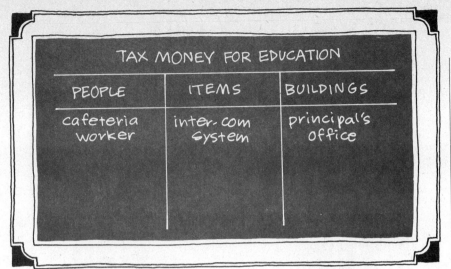

TAX MONEY FOR EDUCATION

PEOPLE	ITEMS	BUILDINGS
cafeteria worker	inter-com system	principal's office

THURS

Objective Associating public services in governmental offices.

Teacher Preparation Lead a brief discussion concerning the various offices of elected officials in city or county government. Place the office names on the chalkboard. Invite at least one official to speak to the class.

Activities Students discuss at least two public services provided from each office.

FRI

Objective Noting the kinds of records kept as a part of public services.

Teacher Preparation Place a time line on the chalkboard, beginning at birth and ending at death. Lead a discussion of the various kinds of public records that might be kept on a person during a lifetime. Have telephone books in the classroom.

Activities For each type of record noted, the students locate the name and telephone number of the appropriate office in the telephone directory for direct information or referral to an office in another city.

Noting Different Aspects of Housing

General Overview There are certain common aspects of housing regardless of where a person lives. In the educational program, study about housing should not be slanted to infer that one type of housing arrangement is better than another; rather, the object is to lead students in discovering basic facts that should be considered.

Learning Objectives Each student will identify ways to best use common housing features, such as furnishings and utilities. In addition, students will study key maintenance factors and analyze features advertised in housing for rent or sale.

MON

Objective Associating budget factors with furnishings.

Teacher Preparation Provide each student with at least two newspapers. Write *$1700* on the chalkboard.

Activities Each student chooses one room in a house (living room, bedroom, den, etc.) and selects advertised furnishings in the newspaper to furnish the room. The cost of the furnishings, including tax, is not to exceed $1700. Students paste the advertisements on a sheet of paper. An extended aspect of this lesson is to compute purchase charge over 24-month and 36-month periods.

TUES

Objective Analyzing utilities in the house from the standpoint of (1) cost and (2) basic versus optional.

Teacher Preparation Lead a brief discussion of the difference between utilities used for basic necessities (heating, water, etc.), and utilities used to operate optional items (electric can opener, electric toaster, electric toothbrush, etc.). Provide each small group of students with a catalog.

Activities Students paste catalog items that are associated with basic uses of utilities (water faucet) on one page and optional items (electric timer) on another page. Then they discuss which ones might be eliminated first if a budget is cut.

WED

Objective Noting facts concerning advertised housing for rent.

Teacher Preparation Provide each pair of students with the newspaper classified advertisements showing housing for rent.

Activities Based on information in the advertisements, students select appropriate rental housing for:

—a family with seven children

—one adult with two pets

—an elderly couple

—a single person who does not have a car

THURS

Objective Noting facts concerning advertised housing for sale.

Teacher Preparation Provide each pair of students with the classified advertisements showing housing for sale.

Activities The students locate one advertisement for each of the following:

—the most expensive house for sale

—the least expensive house for sale

—the largest house for sale

—a house with five bedrooms

—a house with four bedrooms

—a house with several acres of land

—a house still under construction

General Overview The major concept to develop during this week's lesson is that income stretches only so far, and how a person allocates and spends his or her money can be on a sensible or irresponsible basis.

Learning Objectives Each student will study various aspects of monetary budgeting, including developing a personal budget.

FRI

Objective Learning basic housing items that require regular and irregular maintenance.

Teacher Preparation Lead a brief discussion of different large and small housing items, such as *roof, central heating unit, walls, door knobs, window frame,* etc.

Activities For each item identified, students note if the item usually requires repair work. Discuss which are the most expensive repair items.

MON

Objective Learning to prepare a personal budget.

Teacher Preparation Ask each student to pretend his or her income for one week is $5. Collect the papers after the students have completed the activity below.

Activities Each student makes an item budget indicating how the $5 would be spent each week.

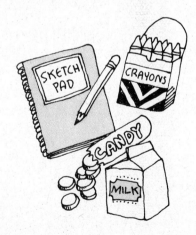

TUES

Objective Noting essential items to include in a budget.

Teacher Preparation Return the budgets prepared on Monday, and ask students to check any money that must be spent each week because the items are essential. If students have not included a savings item, ask them to direct some of the $5 to a weekly savings account. Collect the papers after the students have completed the activity below.

Activities Students indicate at least two essential items in addition to the savings item. (*Note:* The meaning of "essential" should be interpreted individually by each student.)

Notes

WED

Objective Noting extra items to include in a budget.

Teacher Preparation Return the papers collected on Tuesday.

Activities Students note all items that are considered not essential, or extra. They compare the projected total cost of essential items versus extra items in the personal budget.

THURS

Objective Preparing a hypothetical budget for a family.

Teacher Preparation Lead a discussion of major typical budget items in a family of two adults and two children, and write these items on the chalkboard. Write *$12,000* on the chalkboard.

Activities Each pair of students prepares a year's budget based on an income of $12,000 for the family. Beside each item they project the year's cost, and the year's total should not exceed $12,000. If the expenses are greater than the income, the students compute the cost of borrowing the difference at the current interest rate for one year.

FRI

Objective Learning about items in a school budget.

Teacher Preparation Invite the principal to talk to the class about the items in the school budget and the allocated sum for each item.

Activities Students should be encouraged to ask questions.

Notes

Studying about Ecology

General Overview Efforts to maintain the balance of nature are frustrated by people who are careless or thoughtless in ecological matters. In addition to understanding the importance of ecology, students need also to learn what they can and should do. Both factors should be covered in each lesson during the ninth week.

Learning Objectives Each student will associate ecological efforts and factors associated with natural disasters, fires, trash, waters, and living plants.

MON

Objective Learning kinds of restoration efforts needed after natural disasters.

Teacher Preparation Lead a brief discussion of the following major natural disasters: *tornados, hurricanes,* and *forest fires.*

Activities For each item, small groups of students discuss: (1) causes, (2) immediate effects, (3) assistance needed to restore order, and (4) long-range effects.

TUES

Objective Studying fire-protection techniques.

Teacher Preparation Provide each group of students with at least three different references to fire-prevention techniques. Suggested references are: (1) encyclopedia, (2) information in science textbooks, and (3) pamphlets from forestry service.

Activities Students list the suggested techniques in preventing forest fires from each of the printed references. After all the references have been read, students compare the information and decide cn the best reference.

WED

Objective Analyzing ecological effects of trash on streets, vacant lots, and highways.

Teacher Preparation Lead a brief discussion of the kinds of trash found on public property, costs of removing the items, fines, and which items are more dangerous than others.

Activities Each student is encouraged to contribute to the discussion.

THURS

Objective Learning ecological factors associated with lakes and rivers.

Teacher Preparation Provide library books on subjects relating to water ecology. Lead a class discussion of causes and effects of water pollution and treatment procedures.

Activities Each student is encouraged to contribute to the discussion.

FRI

Objective Contributing to ecological efforts.

Teacher Preparation Contact a garden club and ask if a tree or shrub could be donated to the class. Lead a discussion with the students on beautification techniques involving live plants. Invite a garden club member to visit the class to observe the planting and talk with students about care of plants.

Activities Students select a site for the plant and secure the principal's approval of the site. The class plants the tree and holds a "dedication to the school" ceremony.

Notes

10

General Overview Knowledge of various kinds of machine-based transportation vehicles and their direct and indirect effects on a person's life is a primary area in social studies. To supplement each class discussion, the teacher should provide magazines, film strips, films, and photographs containing references to different modes of transportation.

Learning Objectives Each student will discuss and relate to personal life the following forms of machine-based travel: airplane, bus, automobile, train, and ship.

MON

Objective Discerning effects of airborne travel.

Teacher Preparation Provide each pair of students with a magazine. Place the two categories of *people* and *cargo* on the chalkboard.

Activities Each pair of students locates and notes the appropriate column items in the magazine that can or should be transported by air to minimize travel time. In the "People" column, a specific designation (Hawaii, for example) as advertised in the magazine could be noted, along with the reason why air travel might be preferred. In the "Cargo" column, the students note one reason for suggesting air travel, such as shipping perishable foods or transporting animals. Small-group discussions of different types of air travel (private two-person planes, commercial jets, helicopters, seaplanes, etc.) should be held.

TUES

Objective Noting contributions of transportation by bus.

Teacher Preparation Provide each pair of students with a newspaper and a road map of the United States.

Activities Using the city names from which the news stories originated, each pair of students charts a bus trip to include each city. The students compute the approximate number of miles in the shortest route. In small groups, students discuss the kinds of cargo items frequently shipped by bus. (Examples: gift parcels, mail, tools, etc.)

WED

Objective Analyzing contributions of automobile travel.

Teacher Preparation Provide each pair of students with a city map.

Activities Each pair of students plans a weekend vacation trip within the city limits to points of interest indicated on the map. In addition, they locate a motel site, if possible. They mark a logical travel route and compute the approximate number of miles in the trip.

THURS

Objective Noting contributions of transportation by train.

Teacher Preparation Provide each pair of students with a catalog, such as Sears Roebuck, J. C. Penney, Montgomery Ward. Place on the chalkboard two columns: *Carry in Auto from Store*, and *Company Must Ship by Railroad Express*.

Activities The students note in each column at least five items in the catalog. The items in the first column should be light enough to be carried home by a person. In the second column, the students note the cost of shipping heavier items by railroad express.

11

General Overview Constructive use of leisure time often involves more than merely choosing a recreational activity. For most leisure-time activities, there is a financial investment along with reading and writing with reference to the topic. Although some recreational activities can be undertaken alone, others require additional people. In all instances, the selection process is based on enough exposure to, and interest in, the activity to warrant further self-commitment.

Learning Objectives Each student will learn to analyze interest factors associated with various ways to spend leisure time.

FRI

Objective Noting contributions of transportation by ship.

Teacher Preparation Provide each small group of students with travel brochures from at least two different shipping lines, and pamphlets from manufacturers of automobiles made in a foreign country.

Activities The students analyze the travel brochure to compare costs, services, places visited, etc. From the automobile pamphlets, they note the country in which the cars are made and the ports of entry in this country.

Notes

MON

Objective Learning to identify activities and percentage of time spent by each student in leisure activities.

Teacher Preparation Lead a brief discussion of the kinds of hobbies and other uses of leisure time that class members are now engaged in. Place each topic on the chalkboard.

Activities Each pair of students discusses his/her hobbies and determines how much of a typical morning, afternoon, and night is spent in that pursuit.

TUES

Objective Learning to associate kinds of materials necessary to pursue different types of recreational activities.

Teacher Preparation Give each student a list containing at least five different hobbies or other uses of leisure time. Suggested items are *vacations*, *raising tropical fish*, *building models*, and *reading stories*. Lead a brief discussion covering the kinds of materials that are basic to each activity.

Activities Each pair of students compiles a list of materials associated with at least two other hobbies.

WED

Objective Identifying various printed reference materials to gain additional information regarding different types of leisure activities.

Teacher Preparation Use the encyclopedia or other reference books to locate information pertaining to the history of a leisure-time activity such as *baseball*. Show the students the reference materials.

Activities Each student selects at least one leisure-time activity and uses reference materials to learn historical information about the topic.

THURS

Objective Identifying categories of avocational activities that can be undertaken by an individual.

Teacher Preparation Lead a brief discussion of the kinds of leisure-time activities an individual can pursue without others. Place examples, such as *swimming*, *reading*, *sewing* on the chalkboard, and discuss aspects of each that a person performs alone, as well as portions that require assistance from others. Provide each group of students with a magazine.

Activities Each group of students creates a poster containing magazine pictures as well as illustrations drawn by students of leisure-time activities that can be conducted by an individual.

FRI

Objective Identifying categories of avocational activities that require group participation.

Teacher Preparation Follow the procedures described for Thursday's lesson. Suggested discussion topics for leisure-time activities that require several people are: *football, musical groups*, and *showing dogs*.

Activities On the back of the posters created on Thursday, each group of students pastes magazine pictures and student drawings to develop a poster illustrating different categories of leisure activities that require more than one person.

Notes

Discovering Contributions of Sports to Society

General Overview Sports provide direct and indirect contributions to society. For those actively involved, the physical exercise and group cooperation can be beneficial. For nonplayers, sports indirectly provide contributions through recreational outlets for spectators, financial support to various institutions, and income for businesses when trade is gained as a result of sports equipment and events.

Learning Objectives Each student will discover benefits from various kinds of sports, including those benefits gained through involvement of participants and spectators, business transactions, and public support.

MON

Objective Discovering direct benefits to participants.

Teacher Preparation Lead a brief discussion of at least five types of sports, with emphasis on benefits gained by the players. Suggested sports are: *baseball, swimming, basketball, fishing,* and *skiing.*

Activities Students make a list of benefits to players for each type of sport discussed.

TUES

Objective Discovering indirect benefits to spectators.

Teacher Preparation Provide each pair of students with a copy of the sports pages in a newspaper. Have various sports magazines such as *Sports Illustrated, Field and Stream, Football, Karate.*

Activities Students select at least five different sports and for each describe hypothetical reactions from observers. Students contrast (1) spectators watching the sport on television, (2) spectators at the sport site, and (3) fans reading accounts of the sport activity.

WED

Objective Noting travel, shelter, and food areas where businesses benefit from sports.

Teacher Preparation Briefly discuss the fact that sports are big business for some companies. Place these column headings on the chalkboard: *travel, shelter,* and *food.*

Activities Each student writes the name of at least three sports and lists items in the appropriate column for each sport that represent specific sales associated with sporting events. In the *food* column, for example, students might write *peanuts, popcorn, colas, breakfast at a motel, sandwiches,* etc.

THURS

Objective Noting equipment requirements through which businesses benefit from sports.

Teacher Preparation Lead a brief discussion of the various kinds of equipment necessary for a sport such as swimming, golf, and tennis. Provide catalogs of sporting equipment in the classroom.

Activities Each small group develops a list of basic equipment needed for one sport. Both large equipment (swimming pool) and small equipment (goggles) should be included in the list.

FRI

Objective Realizing community contributions to public sports.

Teacher Preparation Lead a brief discussion of the various recreational facilities provided for the public through taxes. Call the local recreation department for information concerning location and offerings of public recreational sites, yearly costs of operation, and schedules of events. Provide each group of students with information selected and a city map.

Activities Students locate public recreational sites on the map; near each map site, they write the kind of recreational facility available.

Notes

Comparing Different Foods

13

General Overview In addition to the need to learn how to select foods from a nutritional standpoint, the economics of purchasing food wisely is a basic item in elementary social studies.

Learning Objectives Each student will learn to detect nutritional values of selected foods, how to analyze food costs, and ways to preserve foods.

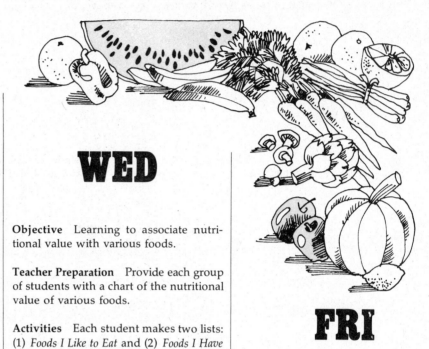

MON

Objective Learning to read ingredients on food labels.

Teacher Preparation Bring to class the labels removed from various food containers. Give each pair of students a stencil copy of the *ingredients* only, without the name of the food.

Activities Students read the ingredients and write the name of the food beside the list of ingredients. Students look at the food labels to check answers.

TUES

Objective Noting different products that have the same food base.

Teacher Preparation Briefly discuss cheese and sour cream as two foods that contain milk and milk products.

Activities Each group of students makes a list of other foods dfrom milk products.

WED

Objective Learning to associate nutritional value with various foods.

Teacher Preparation Provide each group of students with a chart of the nutritional value of various foods.

Activities Each student makes two lists: (1) *Foods I Like to Eat* and (2) *Foods I Have Eaten Recently*. Students use the chart to note the nutritional value beside each item. They compare differences found.

THURS

Objective Noting food costs and changes in food prices.

Teacher Preparation Bring to class empty food containers containing the price of the food. Provide each group of students with several grocery advertisements.

Activities Students compare prices of the same items for sale at different grocery stores, difference in prices advertised and prices marked on the food containers, and any differences in price when buying one item and more than one of the same item.

FRI

Objective Learning various ways to preserve foods.

Teacher Preparation Provide each group of students with a recipe book. Write the following techniques on the chalkboard: *freezing, home canning, drying.*

Activities Each group of students selects at least five recipes, discusses which method(s) can be used to preserve the food, and writes the name of the recipe under the appropriate category or categories.

General Overview Students need to learn to read many different kinds of maps and to note the information in legends and other clarification notations included on maps.

Learning Objectives Each student will learn to locate information on department layouts of large stores, city and state road maps, textbook maps, and house plans.

MON

Objective Making and reading layouts of department stores.

Teacher Preparation Lead a brief discussion of major areas typical in a large clothing store and in a large variety store.

Activities Each student draws a map of either a clothing or variety store and labels the major areas. The student writes three questions pertaining to locating areas on the map and exchanges the map with another student who writes answers to the questions.

TUES

Objective Locating areas on a city map.

Teacher Preparation Provide each small group of students with a copy of a city map. Show students how to find streets on the map.

Activities The students locate the following streets on the map:

1. a street that is a compound word
2. a street that begins with the letter *s*
3. a street that is the name of a person
4. a street that is downtown
5. the street in front of the school

WED

Objective Reading information in text-book maps.

Teacher Preparation Provide students with a textbook that contains maps. Explain map legends and their uses to the students.

Activities Each student selects at least three different maps in the textbook and develops legends to indicate information that: (1) would be helpful to people traveling in an automobile; (2) pertains to climate; (3) pertains to elevation; and (4) pertains to people.

THURS

Objective Locating information on state road maps.

Teacher Preparation Provide each small group of students with a state road map.

Activities The students mark the following on the map: (1) an interstate highway number; (2) a park; (3) a lake; (4) a river; (5) a city of more than 100,000 people; (6) the state capital; (7) a city that is also the name of a food; (8) a city that is also the name of a U.S. president; (9) a city that ends in *ville*.

FRI

Objective Reading house plans.

Teacher Preparation Provide each group of students with a copy of the house plan and furniture shown here, and show them others found in a newspaper, magazine, or book of house plans. Provide scissors and glue.

Activities Students cut out the furniture and arrange it in the appropriate room.

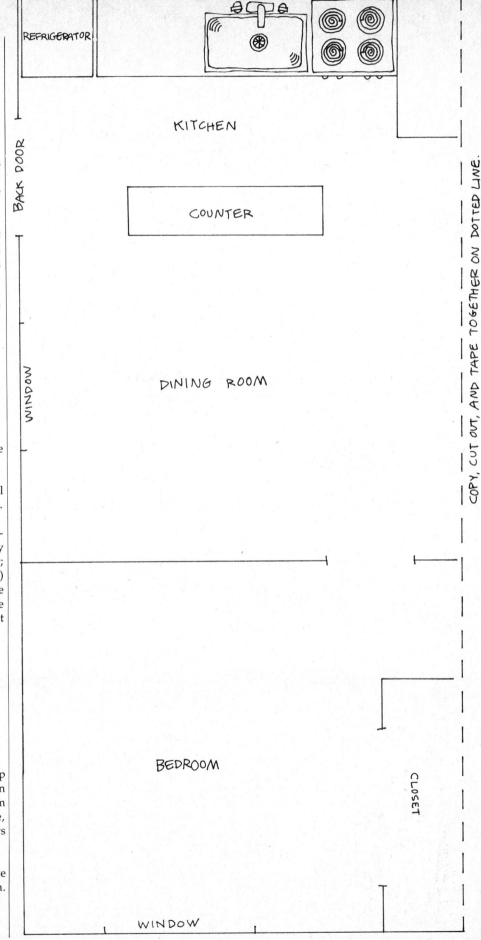

SCALE: ½ INCH = 1 FOOT

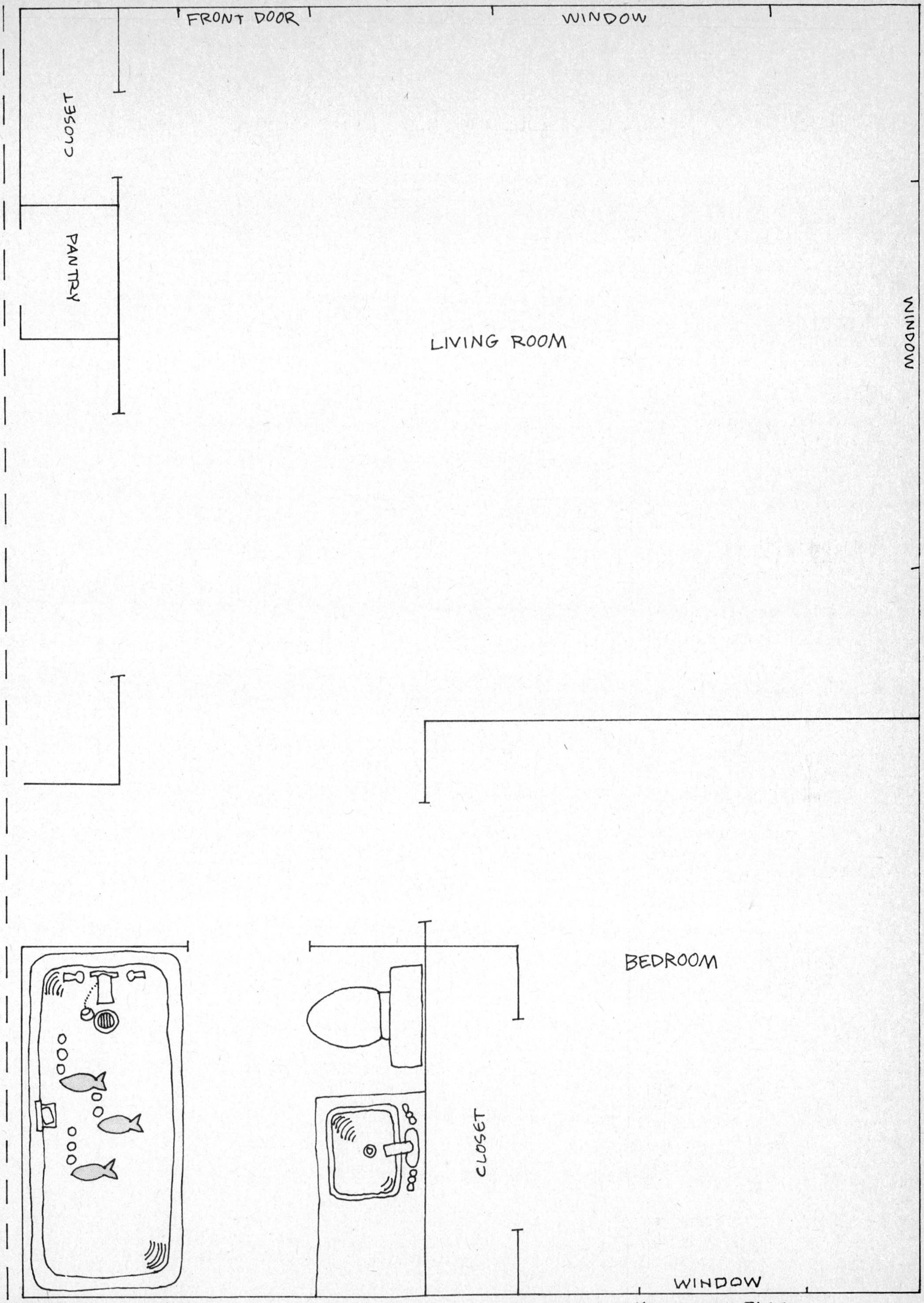
FRONT DOOR
WINDOW
CLOSET
PANTRY
LIVING ROOM
WINDOW
BEDROOM
CLOSET
WINDOW

FURNITURE ON FOLLOWING PAGES

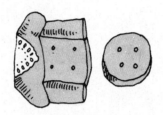
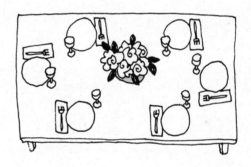

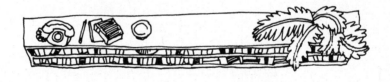

Studying Career Education

15

General Overview In studying various facets of career education, elementary students need to become cognizant of the various job opportunities now present, as well as the underlying theme of changes in occupations. Within each category there are numerous different types of jobs, each requiring specialized skills that may or may not be obsolete by the time these students are adults. During this week, career awareness is emphasized in five categories; however, other areas should be highlighted during the academic year. Provide each student with a large sheet of poster paper divided into five segments—one for each day of the week.

Learning Objectives Each student will associate particular common factors found in the following careers: health services, business and industry, self-employment, public service, and professional careers.

MON

Objective Studying various health-service careers.

Teacher Preparation Provide each pair of students with a list of public services, magazines, and access to a telephone book.

Activities Pairs of students select one health-service area, and in the first block on the poster paper, each pair of students writes one major health-service category, lists different job categories in that area, and pastes appropriate magazine pictures that extend the idea of job category. Display the poster in the classroom.

TUES

Objective Learning about careers in business and industry.

Teacher Preparation Provide each pair of students with the poster that was started on Monday, magazines, newspapers, and access to a telephone book.

Activities Each pair of students selects and writes the name of one business or industry on the Tuesday section of the poster. They write the names of different employee titles typically found in that business, and paste magazine or newspaper pictures that further describe the business in the Tuesday section on the poster before displaying the poster in the classroom.

WED

Objective Learning different self-employment careers.

Teacher Preparation Provide each pair of students with the classified advertisement section of the newspaper, magazines, and their poster.

Activities The students select one category of self-employed businesses as found in the newspaper classified advertisements, and list on Wednesday's segment of the poster the titles of helpers (if any) a person would need to complete the jobs. They add magazine pictures in the Wednesday's section of the poster and post it in the classroom.

THURS

Objective Studying public-service careers.

Teacher Preparation Provide each pair of students with magazines and with access to a telephone book to locate various kinds of public-service offices.

Activities Each pair of students selects one category of public service, and in the Thursday section of the poster, they write the kinds of services provided by that category. Before displaying the poster in the classroom, they add magazine pictures or draw illustrations depicting the various services identified.

FRI

Objective Learning about different self-employed professional careers.

Teacher Preparation Provide each pair of students with magazines, their poster, and a partial list of professional occupations, such as teacher, medical doctor, dentist, lawyer, engineer, and scientist.

Activities Each pair of students selects one professional category and writes titles of supportive personnel with that category on Friday's segment of the poster. They add magazine pictures to further illustrate the concept of the profession. If possible, they locate the minimum number of years a person must be in school past high-school studies before receiving the professional degree.

Notes

Learning Contributions of Different Ethnic Groups

16

General Overview This week's topic is important in the social-studies program. In initiating the study of contributions of various ethnic groups, the teacher should begin with the ethnic background and former nationality (if known) of students in the classroom. In researching the contributions of groups identified, students should be encouraged to work independently as well as in small groups. For each ethnic group, students should locate names of prominent individuals and the reasons for their being famous, as well as significant contributions from the group as a whole. With each lesson, the concept of various groups working with other groups should be stressed. Ethnic groups not represented by the class members should be studied also.

Learning Objectives Each student will learn the names and contributions of at least two famous individuals in the following groups: Blacks, Caucasians, American Indians, Jews, and Mexicans.

MON

Objective Learning contributions of Blacks.

Teacher Preparation Lead a discussion of the contributions of Blacks in the United States. Have biographies about Blacks in the classroom. Provide students with newspapers.

Activities Each student selects the name of at least one famous Black person and, using library books and reference books, locates specific information about this person. Newspapers are used to locate information about Blacks in current events. A general class discussion should be held concerning information found.

TUES

Objective Learning contributions of Caucasians.

Teacher Preparation Lead a class discussion of the contributions of Caucasians in this country. Have biographies about Caucasians in the classroom. Provide each student with newspapers.

Activities Each student selects the name of at least one famous Caucasian and, using library books and reference books, locates specific information about this person. Newspapers are used to locate information about Caucasians in current events. A general class discussion should be held covering information found.

WED

Objective Learning contributions of Indians in the United States.

Teacher Preparation Same as Monday's and Tuesday's lessons except the emphasis is on identification and contributions of Indians in this country.

Activities Same as earlier lessons this week.

THURS

Objective Learning contributions of Jews.

Teacher Preparation Same as earlier lessons this week.

Activities Same as earlier lessons this week.

FRI

Objective Learning contributions of Mexicans.

Teacher Preparation Same as earlier lessons this week.

Activities Same as earlier lessons this week.

Notes

Deemphasizing Sex-Role Stereotypes

General Overview To deemphasize traditional sex stereotypes, lessons should depict females in roles that were formerly shown as masculine, and males in traditional female roles. During the seventeenth week, the lessons emphasize only four areas of changing concepts about sex roles; however, many other topics can be selected for analysis at later dates in the year.

Learning Objectives Each student will identify a male with an occupation formerly reserved for women only, and vice versa.

MON

Objective Learning about males in the kitchen.

Teacher Preparation Lead a brief discussion of times when males assume all cooking responsibilities in the home, and the importance of sharing cooking and house-cleaning chores with females in the family.

Activities Each student in class is asked to cook one meal at home, including setting table, washing dishes, etc.

TUES

Objective Learning about women in heavy construction work.

Teacher Preparation Lead a discussion of erroneous reasons women have not traditionally been employed in construction work. Discuss the legal concept of equal employment.

Activities Each pair of students lists different types of heavy construction work (bricklayer, welder, large-machine operator, etc.) and for each draws a picture with a female performing the job.

WED

Objective Learning about men as secretaries.

Teacher Preparation Lead a class discussion of the past typical roles of females as secretaries and males as "bosses" of the secretaries.

Activities Each pair of students selects a hypothetical business, designs an employee chart, and designates an equal number of males and females for each employee area.

THURS

Objective Learning about women as chief executives in business.

Teacher Preparation Lead a class discussion of the traditional role of the male as chairman, president, executive officer, etc., of a business.

Activities Each student writes a letter to a business requesting information concerning whether the chief officer is male or female, and the title of the highest-ranking female in the business.

18

General Overview Developing a basic understanding and respect for the democratic processes underlying America should include the development of patriotism. For elementary students, specific lessons should emphasize certain rights that the students may take for granted unless they learn that these rights are not present in all countries. Students should realize that the protection and continuation of these rights is a charge of each American.

Learning Objectives Each student will explore selected aspects of patriotism. Specific emphasis is on democratic factors in occupational choices and at home, respect for the American flag, voting rights and responsibilities, and freedom of speech.

FRI

Objective Changing sex stereotypes in other categories.

Teacher Preparation Provide students with magazines and copies of letters from various companies.

Activities Students look at signatures on the letters to discuss if they are masculine or feminine, and note the titles of each. They select magazine pictures and discuss the concept of males in roles depicted in magazines as female and vice versa.

Notes

MON

Objective Discussing elements of democracy in occupational choices.

Teacher Preparation Provide each student with a magazine. Lead a class discussion concerning the differences between a democracy where people have choice in selecting occupations and forms of government where the government decides what jobs will be performed by people.

Activities Each pair of students locates magazine illustrations depicting various forms of occupations and discusses possible reasons those jobs were chosen, as well as various requirements a person must meet to be eligible to perform the job.

TUES

Objective Discussing elements of democracy at home.

Teacher Preparation Lead a class discussion of the right of each person to decide how time is spent in the home, as well as the illegality of searching someone's home without a search warrant. Include in the discussion areas where there are governmental controls, such as taxation on property, building codes, sanitation laws, etc.

Activities Each small group of students makes a list of related items that are free of government control and areas where there are government regulations.

WED

Objective Developing respect for the meanings of the American flag.

Teacher Preparation Provide reference books containing information concerning the history of the American flag.

Activities Each small group of students researches the history of the flag. The class discusses the information found in several different resources.

THURS

Objective Learning about voting rights and responsibilities.

Teacher Preparation Lead a discussion of the difference between living in a country where some politicians are elected to office by the people as contrasted with being in a country where the people have no choice in the governmental leaders. Discuss the responsibility of each American citizen to register to vote and exercise the voting right. Provide each pair of students with a newspaper and access to an encyclopedia.

Activities Students read the newspaper to locate names and titles of elected officials in the news. They use reference books to locate the major functions of offices.

FRI

Objective Learning about freedom of speech.

Teacher Preparation Lead a class discussion of the difference between living in a country where there is freedom of speech as contrasted with living in a country where public information receives censorship before dissemination. Provide small groups of students with several different editorials.

Activities Students read the editorials and underline parts that they think might have been censored if written in a country where information is suppressed.

Detecting Reasons for Conflicts

19

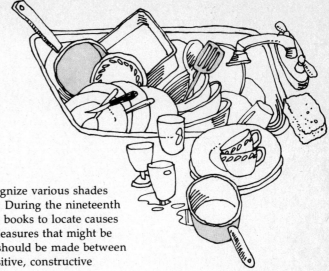

General Overview   Students need to learn not only to recognize various shades of conflicts, but also to detect causes and effects of conflicts. During the nineteenth week, the emphasis is on class discussions, use of reference books to locate causes and effects of past conflicts, and identification of possible measures that might be taken to avoid similar conflicts in the future. A distinction should be made between negative, destructive conflicts (war, riots) as opposed to positive, constructive conflicts (sports, self-improvement efforts).

Learning Objectives   Each student will identify causes and effects of internal self-conflicts and of conflicts found in nature, homes, cities, and between nations.

MON

Objective   Identifying conflicts within one's self.

Teacher Preparation   Place topics such as the following on the chalkboard: *To Study or to Play; To Share or Not to Share Food; To Demand or to Share Attention from Adults; To Perform or Not to Perform Chores at Home.*

Activities   Students discuss various causes of the conflicts and possible effects depending on selections made.

TUES

Objective   Noting positive and negative conflicts in home-based relationships.

Teacher Preparation   Provide each pair of students with a magazine.

Activities   Students locate domestic pictures and for each identify one possible conflict that might arise between family members concerning an idea in the picture. For each conflict, the students suggest a positive solution.

WED

Objective   Noting major conflicts found in cities.

Teacher Preparation   Provide each pair of students with a newspaper.

Activities   The students read articles to locate different kinds of conflicts that occur in a city. They underline the reported causes and effects of the conflicts.

THURS

Objective   Learning about past conflicts between nations.

Teacher Preparation   Provide each pair of students with access to a reference book containing accounts of wars.

Activities   The students identify one war and research printed information to locate causes and effects of the war.

FRI

Objective   Noting conflicts in nature.

Teacher Preparation   Provide each pair of students with access to reference books concerning nature. Discuss natural enemies in categories of *animals, birds, fish,* and *natural events.*

Activities   Students write at least two items in each column that might conflict with each other. They refer to reference books for information.

Notes

Learning about Clothing

20

TO KEEP WARM

General Overview A study of clothing for elementary students involves learning to select appropriate clothing not only for various climatic conditions but also according to costs and material. Since a considerable portion of a budget may be spent for clothing, this topic is basic in social studies.

Learning Objectives Each student will learn to select kinds of clothing needed for winter and summer, note differences between basics and frills in clothing, identify different kinds of fabric and how to care for them, and relate budgetary concerns with clothing needs.

MON

Objective Identifying clothing needed in cold weather.

Teacher Preparation Provide each student with a catalog containing a large assortment of clothing for sale.

Activities Students use the index to locate a basic wardrobe for cold weather. They paste the clothing picture, including price, on paper and beneath each picture they write one reason the article is needed in cold weather.

TUES

Objective Identifying clothing needed in warm weather.

Teacher Preparation Same as Monday's lesson.

Activities Same as Monday's lesson, except the emphasis is on selecting a basic wardrobe to wear in hot weather.

WED

Objective Distinguishing between basic clothing and extras.

Teacher Preparation Provide each student with the posters created on Monday and Tuesday along with a clothing catalog.

Activities For each basic item, the students locate in the catalog and paste beside the item one related "frill" item. (Example: *iron-on tattoos on shirts.*)

THURS

Objective Creating a hypothetical clothing budget.

Teacher Preparation Provide each student with the posters created earlier in the week.

Activities Each student selects the basic clothing items and totals the cost of purchasing one or one pair of each. Students then compute the cost of the extra item and decide which of the extra items they would not purchase if the cost exceeded the clothing budget.

FRI

Objective Learning about the care of different fabrics.

Teacher Preparation List on the chalkboard different fabrics as found on clothing labels. Bring the labels to school and provide each small group of students with several labels.

Activities Students copy the fabrics listed from the chalkboard and, using information from the labels, write beside each fabric the cleaning method as recommended on the label.

Notes

Recognizing Various Kinds of Freedoms

21

General Overview During the eighteenth week, the rights of voting and speech are emphasized. Those points might be used in introductory sessions held this week. In addition, there are numerous other freedoms, each of which can be used effectively or misused. Discerning that difference is a major goal of this week's lessons.

Learning Objectives Each student will explore freedom to write letters, travel, shop, select television programs, and read books.

MON

Objective Learning to discern the difference between using and misusing television.

Teacher Preparation Lead a discussion of the difference between government-owned TV stations and commercial stations. Provide each student with a copy of a television schedule for one week. Discuss causes and effects of watching television to the exclusion of other kinds of activity.

Activities Each pair of students designs a week's schedule of watching TV that seems reasonable.

TUES

Objective Learning about the importance of freedom to write letters.

Teacher Preparation Lead a class discussion of the freedom of individuals to write letters without fear of the letter being opened, read, or perhaps censored. Discuss misuses of the mails.

Activities Each group of students makes a list of different agencies or persons one might write for specific information. Beside each name, the students note a topic of a letter.

WED

Objective Noting aspects of freedom to travel within a city, from city to city, and from state to state.

Teacher Preparation Lead a class discussion of the American freedom to travel without search within this country. Discuss places people cannot enter and reasons for the restriction. Provide each student with a map of several states.

Activities Students plan a travel schedule. They mark on the map any restricted areas they would not enter.

THURS

Objective Noting freedom to shop at a place of one's choice.

Teacher Preparation Lead a class discussion of the right of a person to shop at any store. Discuss limitations, such as budget items, not indicated in a store's wares, etc. Provide each group of students with pamphlets of local businesses, such as those used by the Chamber of Commerce, and the yellow pages of the telephone book.

Activities Each student plans a shopping trip (1) for pleasure and (2) to purchase basic necessities. They write the name and address of each business selected, and one item that might be purchased in that store.

FRI

Objective Noting freedom to read, purchase, or select library books of one's choice.

Teacher Preparation Invite the librarian to talk to the class, emphasizing the varieties of books and topics in the school library. Provide students with telephone books and a local map. Lead a class discussion of the freedoms to read magazines, newspapers, comics, books, etc., and various ways to get reading materials.

Activities Students participate in class discussions with the librarian and teacher. They locate public libraries in the telephone book's yellow pages and find the nearest library site on the map.

Notes

Recognizing Major Purposes of Selected Institutions

22

General Overview Established mechanisms or institutions that promote a global concept affect each person in society. Students need to be aware of the existence of such institutions in their broad sense, and some of the services provided.

Learning Objectives Each student will learn to identify selected types of institutions and to recognize some of their major purposes. Specific institutions studied during this week are: hospitals, corporations, schools, laws, and foundations.

MON

Objective Learning the concept of hospitals as institutions.

Teacher Preparation Lead a class discussion of the difference between having a major hospital, which incorporates several types of health services, and lacking hospital facilities and specialists, in which situation each person would have to provide some semblance of health care. Provide each pair of students with magazines and newspapers.

Activities Students develop a poster entitled *Hospitals as Institutions* using newspaper articles and magazine pictures containing references to persons receiving medical care in hospitals.

TUES

Objective Learning the concept of corporations as institutions.

Teacher Preparation Lead a discussion of the differences between a small operation such as a garage sale and a large business such as General Electric.

Activities Students locate in magazine and yellow pages of the telephone book the names of businesses that are incorporated. They use context clues to note the kinds of services or products provided by the business.

WED

Objective Learning the concept of schools as institutions.

Teacher Preparation Lead a discussion concerning different schools (public, private, elementary, secondary, university, trade, education by mail, etc.). Provide each pair of students with a magazine.

Activities Students discuss reasons why schools exist, and why individuals select certain areas of study to concentrate on while in school. They locate magazine pictures and associate the effects of schools on topics illustrated.

THURS

Objective Discovering the intangible concept of the system of laws as an institution.

Teacher Preparation Of the topics emphasized this week, the system of laws as an institution is the most abstract. Lead a class discussion of topics such as drug abuse, speeding, robbery, and voting.

Activities Student discussions of items on chart.

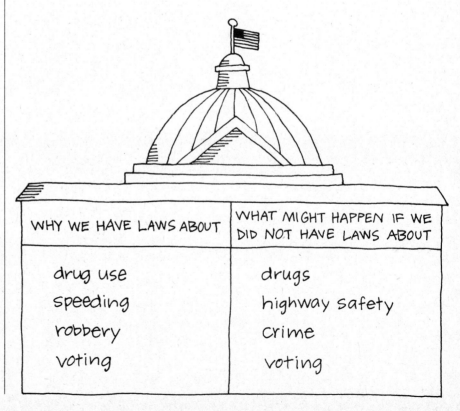

WHY WE HAVE LAWS ABOUT	WHAT MIGHT HAPPEN IF WE DID NOT HAVE LAWS ABOUT
drug use	drugs
speeding	highway safety
robbery	crime
voting	voting

FRI

Objective Learning about foundations as institutions.

Teacher Preparation Lead a class discussion of the concept of charitable foundations. Locate names and addresses of foundations such as Rockefeller, Carnegie, and Ford.

Activities Each student writes one foundation requesting information concerning charitable or research expenditures made by that foundation.

Notes

23

General Overview During one's lifetime, one is directly involved in many different types of groups, either through personal choice or through placement in a group by others. Determining the purpose of the group and how one can best contribute to positive group actions is a basic educational component in social studies.

Learning Objectives Each student will discuss and participate in simulated group processes with specific attention given to group communications in school, business, government, and on a voluntary basis.

MON

Objective Noting the effects of groups on personal conversation.

Teacher Preparation Lead a class discussion of the effects on a person caused by conversations in different kinds of groups.

Activities Each pair of students completes a chart by writing in at least one effect that various group conversations might have on a person.

TUES

Objective Observing groups at work in school.

Teacher Preparation Define various kinds of groups in the school, such as cafeteria workers, second-grade students, visitors, etc.

Activities Each small group of students selects one group and role-plays a conversation among those group members. Other students listen to note any possible effects the comments might have on members of the class.

CONVERSATION BY	POSSIBLE EFFECT ON AN INDIVIDUAL
1 The baseball team	1 _____
2 Family members planning a vacation	2 _____
3 Teachers' meeting at school	3 _____
4 Friends meeting on Saturday morning	4 _____

FRI

Objective Learning about various group processes involving volunteers.

Teacher Preparation Lead a class discussion concerning different types of volunteer groups. Suggested examples are hospital volunteers and tutors.

Activities Small groups role-play different aspects of a volunteer's group process, such as recruitment, training, and on-the-job activities. For each aspect, other students note the various components depicted during the role-playing that represent a group process at work.

Notes

WED

Objective Learning various types of group process in business.

Teacher Preparation Provide each pair of students with a magazine.

Activities The students select one magazine advertisement and discuss the kinds of groups that might have been involved in manufacturing, selling, and purchasing the product. They write group names in a chart.

THURS

Objective Learning about governmental group processes.

Teacher Preparation Lead a class discussion of the major responsibilities of one type of governmental official or agency from the local, state, and national levels. Examples are mayors, governors, highway safety commissioners, tax assessors, etc.

Activities Each group of students defines groups associated with each topic selected and some of the group responsibilities.

PRODUCT

making the product	selling the product	buying the product

Assuming Responsibilities

24

General Overview Dependability in assuming responsibilities is a critical personal characteristic, and exploration of the need for assuming responsibilities to self and to others is one area of social studies that should receive priority attention. Responsibilities of persons in a variety of areas is the focus of the twenty-fourth week.

Learning Objectives Each student will learn to identify selected basic responsibilities that a person has to pets, family, school, community, and self.

MON

Objective Recognizing responsibilities to pets.

Teacher Preparation Provide each pair of students with the "Pets for Sale" column in a newspaper.

Activities Students select one pet advertised and make a list of responsibilities that should be assumed by the owner in caring for the pet.

TUES

Objective Noting responsibilities as family members.

Teacher Preparation Lead a class discussion of various responsibilities assumed by members of the teacher's immediate family to each other. Provide students with magazines.

Activities Each small group of students prepares a poster containing pictures representing parents or guardians and brothers and sisters (at various ages). For each family member, they draw lines connecting the pictures representing those members and write on the lines at least one responsibility to other family members.

WED

Objective Associating responsibilities of students to school.

Teacher Preparation Lead a discussion of the kinds of responsibilities a student has to the school. Write each area mentioned by class members on the chalkboard.

Activities Each student is encouraged to contribute at least one item to be written on the chalkboard.

THURS

Objective Learning responsibilities to the community.

Teacher Preparation Lead a discussion of different areas and groups of people identified in a community. Write each area mentioned by class members on the chalkboard.

Activities Each student is encouraged to choose one area and to tell one way a person can be responsible for the development and maintenance of that topic.

FRI

Objective Identifying responsibilities to self.

Teacher Preparation Ask students to note aspects of self-care for which a person should assume responsibility.

Activities For each area identified, students note one specific way an individual can assume responsibility. For example, *clothing—help keep clothes clean.*

Notes

Learning Various Governmental Operations

25

General Overview During the twenty-fifth week, the emphasis on governmental operations is aimed at three levels: (1) observation of concrete or direct effects of governmental actions; (2) contrast of current governmental decisions with past events; and (3) the overriding concept of the effects of decisions of people in electing and appointing governmental officials.

Learning Objectives Each student will identify evidence of governmental operations in the past and present times. Specific references will be made to the roles Americans have in governmental operations.

MON

Objective Understanding the concept of government "for the people."

Teacher Preparation Lead a class discussion of various responsibilities government has to the American people. Provide each student with a social-studies textbook.

Activities Each student uses the index to locate one item that refers to an area of governmental responsibility to Americans. The student reads that information in the textbook and discusses content found with other members of a small group.

TUES

Objective Understanding the concept of government "of the people."

Teacher Preparation Lead a class discussion of the fact that elected governmental officials are placed in office by Americans through the voting process; appointed governmental officials are usually selected by those who have been elected. Contrast the difference between direct and indirect placement of governmental members by the people of this country. Provide access to reference books.

Activities Each group of students makes a list of governmental officials and uses reference books to find out if these persons in government are elected or appointed.

WED

Objective Understanding the concept of government "by the people."

Teacher Preparation Lead a class discussion of the fact that elected governmental officials represent many different areas of the country, as well as different occupations, economic backgrounds, etc. Contrast this concept with that of a monarchy or dictatorship. Provide students with access to reference books.

Activities Each pair of students selects two United States senators or representatives and contrasts information concerning place of birth and state represented, former occupation, and the like.

THURS

Objective Locating evidence of governmental operations in current events.

Learning Objectives Provide each pair of students with newspapers.

Activities Students locate news articles containing information about decisions and/or actions taken by governmental officials. In the articles, they circle the name and title of the person, and underline references to decisions and/or actions made.

FRI

Objective Locating evidence of governmental operations in American history.

Teacher Preparation Provide each student with social-studies textbooks.

Activities Each student selects the name of a famous governmental official who is no longer living, locates information concerning the role of that person in government, and cites at least two historical events associated with that person.

Notes

Locating Selected Current Events

26

General Overview Keeping abreast of the news is a fundamental aspect of social studies, and elementary students should learn various types of current-events information as well as sources for locating such materials.

Learning Objectives Each student will read and discuss current events, with specific attention given to sports, editorial themes, society news, education, and other countries.

WED

Objective Noting current events in society.

Teacher Preparation Provide each pair of students with front pages of newspapers. Ask students to watch national and local newscasts on television.

Activities With the newspapers, students circle words depicting major events or concerns in different cities as found on the front pages. While watching news broadcasts at home, the students are to make a list of different concerns communicated during the news program.

MON

Objective Reading current events in sports.

Teacher Preparation Provide each group of students with recent issues of sports magazines and sports sections in newspapers.

Activities Each student in the group selects a different sport and locates recent events concerning that sport. The student completes items in chart form.

TUES

Objective Locating current concerns in editorials.

Teacher Preparation Provide each pair of students with at least one editorial from a newspaper or news magazine.

Activities Students circle the words related to the main theme(s) in an editorial, and underline editorial suggestions related to resolving concerns in the editorial.

THURS

Objective Learning information about current events in other countries.

Teacher Preparation Provide each pair of students with newspapers and access to world maps or globes.

Activities Students circle news articles containing information about other countries. They select at least one item and underline the causes and effects of the theme of the news article. They locate the country on a map or globe.

FRI

Objective Finding current events about education.

Teacher Preparation Provide students with newspapers.

Activities Students locate news articles containing information about school-board decisions, interviews with school officials, sports events at different schools, new curriculum programs, and the like. Each student also interviews at least one person in the school and writes an education news article to include in a "newspaper" to be disseminated by the class.

SPORT	PEOPLE IN NEWS	PLACE THE SPORT IS PLAYED	EVENTS THAT HAPPENED	RESULTS OF THE GAME

27

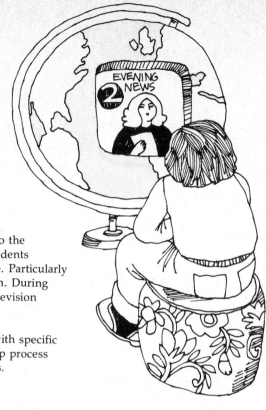

General Overview Educators must incorporate television offerings into the educational programs rather than ignore the impact of television on students as well as the vast amount of time spent by students watching the tube. Particularly in social studies, television offers much for the social-studies curriculum. During this week, at least one assignment will be given each night to watch television for a specific program.

Learning Objectives Each student will associate watching television with specific educational purposes, such as historical and geographical studies, group process in action, results of different occupations, and assuming responsibilities.

MON

Objective Watching television to locate evidence from the past.

Teacher Preparation Provide students with television schedules of tonight's programs. Discuss which ones might contain references to different historical periods.

Activities Students watch a television program and take notes of specific references to different historical periods.

TUES

Objective Contrasting different geographical locations as shown on television.

Teacher Preparation Provide students with the schedule of tonight's television programs, and discuss possible geographical locations of programs.

Activities Students watch television and take notes of country, state, city, and other geographical locations such as rivers, desert, etc. shown on the program.

WED

Objective Noting effects of groups working and playing together as shown on television.

Teacher Preparation Lead a class discussion of different kinds of groups shown on different television programs. Provide students with a schedule of tonight's television program and discuss which groups might be shown.

Activities Students watch television and take notes of the various different groups shown working together.

THURS

Objective Observing different occupations as shown on television.

Teacher Preparation State the names of various popular evening television programs and lead a class discussion of different occupations that have been shown on those programs. Provide students with a schedule of tonight's programs.

Activities Students watch television and list occupations depicted.

GEOGRAPHICAL LOCATIONS OF PROGRAMS				
PROGRAM	COUNTRY	STATE	CITY	GEOGRAPHICAL DETAILS
Rhoda	U.S.A.	New York	New York	Big City

FRI

Objective Observing evidence of selection and completion of responsibilities.

Teacher Preparation Lead a class discussion of television characters and evidence of their acceptance or lack of acceptance of responsibility. Provide students with a copy of tonight's television programs.

Activities Students list television characters by name and beside each one indicate if a responsibility assumed was completed during the program.

Notes

28

General Overview Elementary students need to be aware of various aspects of the history of different ethnic groups. Within each group there are key leaders, historical events, and contributions that distinguish one group from others.

Learning Objectives Each student will learn selected historical information about different ethnic groups. Specific attention will be given to leaders, historical sites, holidays, and unique contributions.

MON

Objective Locating selected information about Blacks.

Teacher Preparation Provide each student with reference books and a copy of this chart. Collect the charts at the end of today's session.

Activities Ask the students to work in groups as well as individually to place on the chart at least two items in each column entry about Blacks.

TUES

Objective Locating selected information about Caucasians.

Teacher Preparation Give each student reference books and his or her copy of the chart used in Monday's lesson.

Activities The student places on the chart at least two items in each column entry about Caucasians before returning the chart to the teacher.

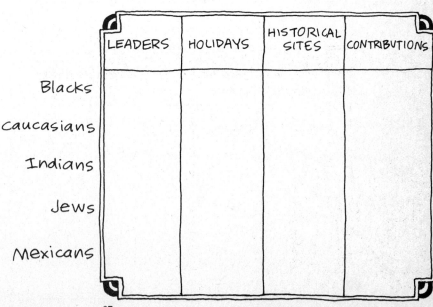

	LEADERS	HOLIDAYS	HISTORICAL SITES	CONTRIBUTIONS
Blacks				
Caucasians				
Indians				
Jews				
Mexicans				

WED

Objective Locating selected information about American Indians.

Teacher Preparation Give each student reference books and his or her chart.

Activities The student places on the chart at least two items in each column entry about American Indians before returning the chart to the teacher.

THURS

Objective Locating selected information about Jewish people.

Teacher Preparation Give each student reference books and his or her copy of the chart.

Activities The student places on the chart at least two items in each column entry about Jews before returning the chart to the teacher.

FRI

Objective Locating selected information about Mexican-Americans.

Teacher Preparation Give each student reference books and his or her copy of the chart.

Activities The student places on the chart at least two items in each column entry about Mexicans before returning the chart to the teacher.

Notes

HISTORIC CONTRIBUTIONS		
	males	females
Aviation	Howard Hughes	Amelia Earhart
Science	Albert Einstein	Madame Curie

29

General Overview Traditional social-studies textbooks have emphasized contributions of males, and it is difficult to find numerous references to the contributions made by females in history, economics, politics, etc. Elementary students need to learn that both females and males have played major as well as minor roles in the past and present. During this week, numerous reference books will be needed in the classroom.

Learning Objectives Each student will identify the names and contributions of both females and males in areas such as science, government, education, aviation, and business.

MON

Objective Learning about females and males who have made significant contributions to science.

Teacher Preparation Provide a variety of science reference books and books about scientists.

Activities Students refer to books to locate names and achievements of females and males. They write letters to scientific organizations, if necessary, to obtain information about outstanding females in science.

TUES

Objective Learning about females and males who have made significant contributions to government.

Teacher Preparation Provide a variety of history books and other reference material containing governmental information.

Activities Students search the information to locate names and contributions of both females and males in government.

WED

Objective Learning about females and males who have made significant contributions to education.

Teacher Preparation Lead a class discussion of the roles of various females and males in education. If necessary, refer to a book on history of education for specific names of contributors.

Activities Students in small groups list the names and contributions of adult males and females in the school.

THURS

Objective Learning about females and males who have made significant contributions to aviation.

Teacher Preparation Provide reference materials covering aviation topics, history, etc.

Activities Students locate names and contributions of females and males with reference to aviation. At least one female, Amelia Earhart, should be included. Students write letters to major airlines asking for information concerning the number of females/males who are pilots, captains, flight attendants, etc.

FRI

Objective Learning about females and males who have made significant contributions to business.

Teacher Preparation Provide copies of magazines such as *Business Week* in the classroom.

Activities Students search the magazines to locate names of females and males who are cited as business leaders. They write letters to various businesses, asking for charts or other information of the ratio and rank of females and males in job allocations.

Notes

30

General Overview Learning historical reasons for major dates, including holidays, is an important aspect of social studies. Collect several different calendars that contain holiday notations, and note the variety of types of holidays. Five types are suggested for study this week; supplement these types with others found on the calendars, from interests of members of the class, and from history books.

Learning Objectives Each student will learn historical information about the following types of dates: education milestones, famous persons, historical events, religious observances, and recreational holidays.

MON

Objective Learning selected dates in education.

Teacher Preparation Lead a discussion of some of the major events in education, such as the first kindergarten, Brown decision, first high school, first land-grant college, etc.

Activities Students use reference books to find information, including dates, concerning each topic discussed.

TUES

Objective Studying dates commemorating selected famous people.

Teacher Preparation Provide students with cancelled postage stamps showing pictures of people.

Activities Students use reference materials to locate information concerning the persons, and major dates associated with those persons' lives.

WED

Objective Associating selected historical events with dates.

Teacher Preparation Provide calendars containing holiday notations and postage stamps containing references to famous events.

Activities Students use reference books to locate dates associated with the events pictured on the stamps, and paste the stamps on the appropriate day in the calendar. They write the year beneath the stamp.

THURS

Objective Learning reasons for selected religious events.

Teacher Preparation Provide reference books containing information concerning different religions.

Activities Students locate at least three major religious dates for each of three different religions.

FRI

Objective Learning reasons for national holidays.

Teacher Preparation Provide calendars containing holiday notations and reference books.

Activities Students mark all dates that are observed, in part, by closing school or governmental offices. Each pair of students selects at least one national holiday and locates historical information about that holiday.

Notes

Detecting Propaganda

31

General Overview Influencing opinions through propaganda is an integral aspect of social studies. Elementary students should be able to identify various propaganda techniques and to interpret counterpoints that are not stated.

Learning Objectives Each student will locate, discuss, and interpret opposing viewpoints to propaganda communicated through political cartoons, historical events, advertisements, entertainment descriptions, and business brochures.

MON

Objective Interpreting propaganda in cartoons.

Teacher Preparation Provide each pair of students with a cartoon from a newspaper.

Activities The students read the caption and (1) write a different caption supporting the major ideas in the cartoon, and (2) write a caption opposing the ideas in the cartoon.

TUES

Objective Analyzing propaganda from two sides regarding an historical event.

Teacher Preparation Lead a discussion of at least three major wars. Provide students with access to reference material covering those events.

Activities Students locate information supporting the activities of two opposing nations in each war. They design posters representing viewpoints that might have been held by both sides.

WED

Objective Locating propaganda in advertisements.

Teacher Preparation Provide each student with at least three magazine or newspaper advertisements.

Activities Student circle all words and illustrations in each advertisement that do not *directly* represent the product or its appearance.

THURS

Objective Analyzing propaganda devices in entertainment and recreational areas.

Teacher Preparation Provide students with a list of the following types of communication: restaurant advertisements, movie descriptions, television advertisements, public and private recreational brochures, etc.

Activities Students delete all descriptive words and pictures from the information and compare the result with the original material.

FRI

Objective Detecting propaganda in business information.

Teacher Preparation Provide brochures from places such as Chamber of Commerce, banks, motels, hotels, factories, etc.

Activities Each pair of students reads at least one brochure and deletes all words, phrases, and sentences that are considered more than basic, factual information about the business.

Notes

Learning Contributions of Selected Occupations

32

General Overview With society there are broad categories of groups whose members may have different jobs, but whose ultimate efforts relate to total group contributions. During this week, five such groups are suggested for study, and emphasis should be placed on identifying different names given to group members, their expertise, and how each contributes to that group's efforts.

Learning Objectives Each student will learn to identify and associate groups within groups in the following major categories: construction, education, medicine, law, and recreation.

MON

Objective Noting contributions of those in construction work.

Teacher Preparation Lead a discussion concerning the building trades, including both large-scale construction in cities as well as small-scale ''puttering'' at home.

Activities For each area identified, students name one person and identify a typical role played in constructing the items. Students then illustrate how one person relates to another person in overall construction efforts in society.

TUES

Objective Learning contributions of educators.

Teacher Preparation Place the names of different jobs in education on the chalkboard. Suggested names are: teachers, principals, superintendents, supervisors, and reading specialists.

Activities Students identify one specific contribution of each group as a whole and one way a member of each group contributes to education.

WED

Objective Learning contributions of people associated with medicine.

Teacher Preparation Use the procedure described for Tuesday's lesson, except the groups should be associated with medical care. Suggested groups are: doctors, nurses, medical researchers, veterinarians, and laboratory technicians.

Activities Use the same type of activities as in Tuesday's lesson.

THURS

Objective Learning contributions of people concerned with law.

Teacher Preparation Discuss titles and contributions of groups such as lawyers, chiefs of police, detectives, highway patrolmen, highway commissioners, judges, and court clerks.

Activities Follow the same type of activities as in Tuesday's lesson.

FRI

Objective Learning contributions of persons in recreational groups.

Teacher Preparation Provide sports magazines and sports pages from newspapers.

Activities Students identify different types of groups associated with recreation, names of members of various groups, and at least one way in which each group contributes to society.

Notes

Detecting Messages

33

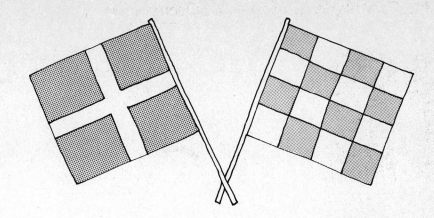

General Overview People receive various types of messages with different degrees of intensity and from numerous sources. In social studies, elementary students need to develop an awareness of both source and intent of various messages.

Learning Objectives Each student will learn to identify and react to messages involving a primary emphasis on body motions, symbols, handwritten notations, emotionally charged messages, and factual information.

MON

Objective Detecting body motions as messages.

Teacher Preparation Ask each student to convey a message using body language.

Activities Each student uses an expression or motion to convey a message; other students guess the message.

TUES

Objective Interpreting messages through symbols.

Teacher Preparation Provide various symbols in the classroom. Suggested symbols are skull and crossbones for poison or danger, red cross, blue cross, highway signs, etc.

Activities Each student interprets the symbol and uses it in a creative writing effort.

WED

Objective Evaluating different types of handwritten notices.

Teacher Preparation Discuss various reasons people leave handwritten messages for others to read.

Activities Each student writes one note, exchanges with another student, and decides whether sufficient information has been given in the message.

THURS

Objective Detecting emotionally charged messages.

Teacher Preparation Provide comic books and newspapers in the classroom.

Activities Each student locates illustrations in the comic book that convey an emotion and discusses with another student both the emotion and degree of possible impact. Repeat the procedure using selected photographs in a newspaper.

FRI

Objective Noting factual messages.

Teacher Preparation Provide social-studies textbooks in the classroom.

Activities Students locate at least three different items of information in the social-studies textbook and compose three "telegrams," each containing major facts.

Notes

Learning Why Selected Places Are Considered Important

34

General Overview For a variety of reasons, and to different degrees, people are affected by the types of places to which they have access. Social studies should include lessons designed to develop awareness of the human purposes served by places and the various actions that take place in different kinds of places.

Learning Objectives Each student will identify and discuss the significance of at least one of the following places: historical sites, businesses, offices, transportation centers, and geographical features.

MON

Objective Identifying reasons for selected historical sites.

Teacher Preparation Provide road maps containing references to historical sites and access to reference books.

Activities Each student selects one historical site and, using reference material, locates information explaining why the area has been so designated.

TUES

Objective Noting different purposes of various kinds of businesses.

Teacher Preparation Provide students with yellow pages from a telephone directory.

Activities Each small group of students "develops" a shopping center containing different kinds of businesses. For each, an explanation should be given concerning why that business should be included in a shopping center. The students then select at least four businesses that should not be in a shopping center and explain why.

WED

Objective Identifying reasons for locations of selected different offices.

Teacher Preparation Lead a discussion of the different kinds of professions that operate from offices.

Activities Students design an office building, naming and explaining at least one service provided by each type of office.

THURS

Objective Discerning reasons for various kinds of transportation centers.

Teacher Preparation List on the chalkboard different kinds of transportation, such as airplanes, private automobiles, commercial bus, taxicabs, rental cars, subways, ships, trains, helicopters, bicycles, etc.

Activities Students discuss where each is usually centered or located and give reasons for both location and services provided.

FRI

Objective Noting effects of geographical locations.

Teacher Preparation Provide maps in the classroom. Write the following on the chalkboard: *lake, river, desert, mountain, beach, swamp,* etc.

Activities Students use the maps to locate as many of the different geographical areas as can be found. They discuss one direct effect people might experience by living in each of the areas.

Notes

35

General Overview People, places, and contributions are three basics associated with learning about another country. During this week each group of two students should select a country, and no two groups should select the same country. Information found during the week should be displayed on classroom walls, and new information should be posted each day.

Learning Objectives Each student will post information concerning geographical features, famous dates, famous people, foods, and industries of another country.

MON

Objective Identifying major geographical features.

Teacher Preparation Provide maps, atlases, and other reference materials in the classroom.

Activities Each pair of students draws an outline map of the country selected, notes neighboring countries, and places on the map at least three major rivers, mountain ranges, or other geographical features found in the country.

TUES

Objective Learning the reasons for selected famous dates.

Teacher Preparation Provide reference materials related to the countries being studied.

Activities Students locate at least five important dates with reference to the country's history. They draw a picture to illustrate the concept of each date.

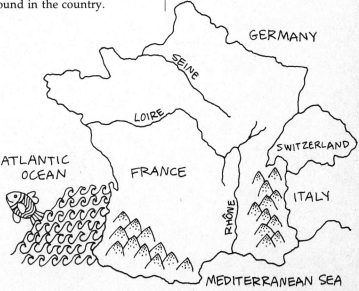

WED

Objective Identifying contributions of heroes.

Teacher Preparation Provide reference materials related to the countries being studied.

Activities Students select at least five national heroes (other than any associated with information found in Tuesday's lesson) and prepare an "advertisement" containing reasons each person is considered famous.

THURS

Objective Noting favorite foods associated with the country.

Teacher Preparation Provide reference materials associated with the countries being studied.

Activities Students prepare a one day's set of meals containing foods that are typical to the country.

FRI

Objective Identifying major industries.

Teacher Preparation Provide reference materials associated with the countries being studied.

Activities Students create a "Jobs Available" section of newspaper classified advertisements. There should be at least five different advertisements, describing five industries, locations, and products a person might be employed to help produce.

Notes

36

General Overview A ''major event'' to one person may be inconsequential to another. In social studies, lessons should be held emphasizing reasons some people consider events major. During this week, broad categories of types of events should be identified by the students with specific happenings that are meaningful to them.

Learning Objectives Each student will identify major events and give at least one reason the events are considered significant.

MON

Objective Identifying major sports or recreation events.

Teacher Preparation Provide sports literature, including the sports section of a newspaper, sports magazines, sports cards, etc.

Activities Each student selects one major event in national sports, or an event that happened this year on the school campus, and writes or discusses why that event is considered significant.

TUES

Objective Identifying major events with reference to one's family.

Teacher Preparation Tell the class about a major event in the teacher's family.

Activities Each student identifies at least two different kinds of positive major events that have happened in his or her family during that student's lifetime.

WED

Objective Identifying major events in this country's history.

Teacher Preparation Provide American history books in the classroom.

Activities Each student selects one event from American history that he/she considers major, and notes reasons for the selection of that event.

THURS

Objective Identifying major events in the history of the city or county in which students now live.

Teacher Preparation Discuss past events in the history of the city or county.

Activities Each student selects at least one major event discussed, and makes a drawing interpreting the causes and effects of that event as perceived by the student.

FRI

Objective Identifying major events that occurred at school this year.

Teacher Preparation Lead a class discussion of various highlights of the school year.

Activities Each student tells or writes an account beginning: ''I am glad I was at school the day _____ happened because _____.''

Notes

Notes

Notes

Notes

Notes